THE OAKWOOD LIBRARY OF RAILWAY HIST

Sir Vincent Raven

and the
North Eastern Railway

by
Peter Grafton

THE OAKWOOD PRESS

© Oakwood Press & Peter Grafton 2005

British Library Cataloguing in Publication Data
A Record for this book is available from the British Library
ISBN 0 85361 640 X

Typeset by Oakwood Graphics.
Repro by Ford Graphics, Ringwood, Hants.
Printed by Cambrian Printers, Aberystwyth, Ceredigion.

For Sally
with love

Raven class 4-6-0 (by this date reclassified as a 'B16/1') No. 61459 of 1923 vintage gave almost 40 years of service. This view shows it in its final years on a permanent way train.
Clive Field Archive

Title page: The first Raven Pacific, No. 2400 *City of Newcastle*, prior to taking part in the 1925 Centenary procession. *John Clewley*

Front cover: Raven 'S2' class 4-6-0 No. 825 with its Stumpf 'Uniflow' cylinders. It was rebuilt with normal cylinders in 1924. *John Alsop Collection*
Rear cover, top: 1,100 hp Bo-Bo electric locomotive No. 3, built for the Shildon-Erimus yard, Newport electrification scheme in 1914, seen here in the paint shop yard at Darlington.
John Alsop Collection
Rear cover, bottom: Raven 'Z' class 4-4-2 No. 727 takes water at Haymarket shed, Edinburgh. This engine was rebuilt in 1931 with a 'booster', making it a 4-4-4, and was withdrawn in 1943. *John Alsop Collection*

Published by The Oakwood Press (Usk), P.O. Box 13, Usk, Mon., NP15 1YS.
E-mail: sales@oakwoodpress.co.uk
Website: www.oakwoodpress.co.uk

Contents

A group of railway staff pose proudly in front of 'T2' class 0-8-0 No. 1257.
John Alsop Collection

Preface

It would be incorrect to state that Sir Vincent Raven's contribution to the development of British railways has been ignored but it has certainly been overlooked and this biography will, it is hoped, re-dress the imbalance.

During the time that the book has been in preparation, I have spent hours at The Public Record Office (now the National Archives), Kew and at The Family Record Centre, Islington and I have found the staff at each location unfailingly helpful, courteous and efficient.

Of necessity I have used the works of other writers as a source of research material and I have acknowledged this either in the Bibliography or in the text. Should I have inadvertently omitted a reference, I apologise.

I have had two indefatigable research assistants who have not only been 100 per cent reliable but also 110 per cent enthusiastic. Jean Earle of Darlington has looked after the 'Darlington end' and my wife Sally who has been a source of inspiration. In fact she became so enthusiastic - especially on our visits to the Public Record Office - that at one stage in the development I felt that the cover should carry her name!

Local historians in and around Hook - Nigel Bell, Ron Brown and Edwina Hancock - have been most helpful as have the staffs of Fleet and Basingstoke libraries. The Reverend Canon Brian Cole not only turned out at short notice on a very hot July day to open All Saints', Great Fransham but also gave unrestricted access to every aspect of the church.

The assistance of members of the North Eastern Railway Association has been invaluable especially Jim Armstrong, George Hearse, John Proud, David Williamson and Dr Geoffrey Hughes who has been most helpful in passing to me information on Raven that he acquired whilst researching his biography of Sir Nigel Gresley and in allowing me to quote from his work on the LNER. Peter Townend whom I have known for more than 30 years has been helpful as ever in supplying information particularly on the pupil/premium apprentice system and allowing me to quote from his writings.

John Coupland Head of Library Services, Institute of Electrical Engineers was instrumental in pointing me in the direction of Raven's paper on Middlesbrough Dock.

Peter Grafton
Paignton
Devon

Chapter One

Great Fransham and School

The following appeared in volume three of the 1925-1940 edition of *Who Was Who*:

Raven, Sir Vincent Litchfield
M.I.C.E., M.I.Mech.E., M.I.E.E.
M 1892 Gifford Chrichton: one s: two d.
Tech adviser LNER 1923:
New South Wales and New Zealand Rlys report 1924
JP Darlington President I.Mech E 1925
Publications - *Middlesbrough Docks*: papers on electric railways, locomotives and traction
Natley Lodge, Hook, Hants: d Felixstowe 14 February 1934.

This brief and understated entry fails to do justice to Vincent Raven who was, arguably, one of the far-sighted - if not the most far-sighted - of the Victorian railway engineers. His work on steam locomotives was overshadowed by Churchward of the Great Western Railway (GWR) and by Gresley of the Great Northern Railway (GNR) but in promulgating his ideas on electric traction, in common with Sir Isaac Newton, he stood on the shoulders of giants.

The hamlet of Great Fransham lies to the east of Swaffham in Norfolk and it was in the rectory of the village - as it was at the time - that Vincent Litchfield Raven was born on 3rd December, 1859, the second of 10 children, to Jemima, the wife of the Reverend Vincent Raven who was appointed Rector of All Saints', Great Fransham in 1853 having previously held livings in places as diverse as Hammersmith and Hackney. Vincent senior had a life-long connection with Magdalen College, Cambridge and the benefice of Great Fransham was in the gift of Magdalen and to be appointed to the living, following Hackney, must have been, literally, a breath of fresh air. He died, still in office, in 1887 having served the parish for 35 years and not having shown any inclination to move. Both Great Fransham and All Saints' Church have been the subjects of social change since Raven's time. The village has lost its station, post office and shop and its pub and All Saints' has lost its full-time incumbent. It is of typical East Anglian construction, flint and freestone, with a 14th century tower surmounted by a squat wooden spire encased in lead. The church was made a Chapel of Ease in 1962 and although it is still used for weddings, funerals and baptisms and has Sunday services once every month, it is, nevertheless, fighting for its survival. The fabric is need of attention and, reading between the lines, the church has never fully recovered from the effects of a flying bomb that landed in a nearby field in 1944. The parishioners are determined that All Saints', with its rich history and its association with Lord Nelson, will be restored and as English Heritage has shown an interest, the future of All Saints', whilst not secure, is brighter than it was. By contrast, the former rectory is alive and well. It is incorporated in The Old Rectory Farm and whilst additions have been made, the original building is clearly discernible.

All Saints' church, Great Fransham.   *Sally Grafton*

The Old Rectory, Great Fransham. Raven's birthplace now part of Rectory Farm.

Sally Grafton

During his incumbency the Reverend Raven must have lived the life of a stereotypical Victorian country parson. That he was not hard pressed so far as his parochial duties are concerned can be deduced from parish registers and from the fact that, as an accomplished woodcarver, he produced the lectern, the pew ends and the altar table shown in the photographs. Village folklore has it that parties of undergraduates from Magdalen would visit the rectory during the summer holidays and be entertained to a touch of country life by the Rector and Mrs Raven. Great Fransham and its neighbouring villages are set in almost idyllic surroundings and one can imagine that it must have been a delightful place for Vincent junior to spend his childhood. In his later years when he 'qualified' for an entry in *Who's Who* he gave his interests as shooting and fishing, no doubt stemming from his time at Great Fransham.

As was the custom amongst the Victorian middle class, the boys were sent away to school whilst the girls were educated at home. Vincent junior was no exception and from the age of seven attended a private school in Brighton. At the age of 11, and accompanied by his elder brother Henry, he went to Aldenham School. Aldenham is a minor public school, founded in 1549 and endowed by the Brewer's Company at a time when it was not uncommon for the Livery Companies to endow schools. Some of the foundations are still very much alive - Dauntsey's, founded by the Mercers Company is an example. Information kindly supplied by the Headmaster of Aldenham school states quite categorically that Raven was at Aldenham from 1870 to 1871. This suggests that he was barely 12-years-old when he left. As his association with the North Eastern Railway did not begin until 1875 one wonders what he was doing in the intervening years. This is not the only anomaly in the Raven canon. The editions of *Who's Who* that were published towards the end of his life list one son and two daughters, and gave the date of his marriage as 1892, but it is established beyond all doubt that he and Lady Raven had two sons and three daughters.

It is possible that Vincent senior's interest in woodcarving - essentially a hands on approach - might have influenced young Vincent in his interest in things practical. At the time that Vincent and Henry were travelling to and from school, Great Fransham was on the North Norfolk line of the GER between Norwich (Thorpe) and Wells-next-the-Sea and the boys would travel firstly to Brighton and latterly to Hertford via Norwich (Thorpe) to Liverpool Street, thence to King's Cross. Vincent jnr would have seen and heard several types of locomotives on his travels from the creations of S.W. Johnson and W. Adams on the Great Eastern Railway (GER) to Patrick Stirling's magnificent 'Singles' on the Great Northern Railway. Add a schoolboy fascination with steam to an inclination towards being practical, then the shaping of Vincent junior's future begins to appear credible. But this is pure speculation and the question of why he travelled so far from home to work for the North Eastern Railway (NER) if, as was the case, he was determined on a railway career, when Stratford and Doncaster were so much nearer, remains unanswered.

Alfred Leeman had been Head at Aldenham nearly 30 years when Henry and Vincent junior arrived in 1870. Their respective careers at the school were uneventful and Vincent junior left in 1871. In 1875 he took up a pupil

Detail of pew end carved by Revd Vincent Raven. *Sally Grafton*

Lectern carved by Revd Vincent Raven. *Sally Grafton*

Altar table made by Revd Vincent Raven. The inscription reads, 'This table is presented to the church of Fransham Magna in loving memory of the Revd Vincent Raven (by whom it is carved) by his widow and children. He fell asleep 12 Decr 1887 aged 72. He was 35 years Rector of this parish'. *Sally Grafton*

An aerial view of Aldenham School. Somewhat different from what Vincent and brother Henry attended. *Courtesy The Headmaster, Aldenham School*

apprenticeship with Edward Fletcher, locomotive superintendent, North Eastern Railway Company at Greenesfield Works, Gateshead. The year 1875 was, according to the minute books, a busy one for the NER. There were several petitions to the Board for lines to be constructed and/or extended, proposals for a tunnel under the river Tees and a strongly worded plea from Joseph Pease for the provision of a Cleveland mineral line. A complaint from Scarborough residents about excessive smoke being emitted by NER locomotives was referred to Mr Fletcher and he was also called upon to report on an accident at Birtley as a result of which the 'permanent way was much damaged'. It seems that an axle on a private owner's goods wagon fractured and that the owner claimed that as all the axles had been renewed, the failure of the axle in question was not his fault. Fletcher reported to the Board that in his opinion the private owner had wasted time and money as the original axles were superior to the

NORTH EASTERN RAILWAY

· DARLINGTON · AUGUST, 1875.

THE DIRECTORS of the NORTH-EASTERN RAILWAY COMPANY having determined to celebrate, at DARLINGTON, on the 27th of SEPTEMBER next, the FIFTIETH ANNIVERSARY of the OPENING of the STOCKTON AND DARLINGTON RAILWAY (the First Public Railway), and having Appointed a Committee to make the requisite Arrangements, I, as Chairman of that Committee, have the pleasure to Invite your Presence and Co-operation.

The Programme is as yet incomplete, but will embrace a Banquet at Darlington on the Evening of the 27th September next, and Visits to Places of Industrial Interest on the following day.

Trusting that the high interest attaching to this Event may induce you to forward to me at an early Day an Acceptance of this Invitation,

I am,

Yours faithfully,

Henry Pease

To

RAILWAY JUBILEE BALL

1825   1875

IN connection with the celebration of the FIFTIETH ANNIVERSARY of the OPENING of the STOCKTON AND DARLINGTON RAILWAY, it is proposed to hold a Ball on the Evening of the 28th inst. in the Banqueting Marquee on the Cricket Ground, Feethams.

The Band of the Grenadier Guards, under the leadership of Mr. DAN GODFREY, has been specially retained for the occasion.

Tickets (Gentlemen, £1 1s., Ladies, 10s. 6d.,) may be had on application to the Honorary Secretaries.

JON E. BACKHOUSE,
RICHARD LUCK, JUN., } Hon. Sec.

DARLINGTON, *September 14th,* 1875.

replacements. Also in 1875 the minutes record three instances of drivers passing signals at danger in January alone, illustrating that passing signals at danger is not a 20th/21st century phenomenon.

Contracts were awarded to 20 suppliers for coal at prices varying from 10s. to 13s. 3d. per ton. One of the contractors was the Revd E. Lawson who tendered to supply 2,000 tons - there is no record of how he came by the coal. Bolckow, Vaughan & Company were invited to tender for the supply of 1,000 tons of rails as a matter of urgency and another matter that was exercising the Board was the charges for the 'conveyance of horses for the Yeomanry and the Volunteers'.

The name of Bolckow, Vaughan & Company recurs in the minutes as the company was amongst the NER's best customers. The production figures for 1874 were published in 1875 - 1,119,251 tons of pig iron and most of it transported by the NER. H.W.F. Bolckow and 'Johnny' Vaughan were the Founding Fathers of the iron and steel industry on Teesside and built what is generally acknowledged to be the first new town - Middlesbrough, known to the Victorians as 'Ironopolis'. All this was going on around the young Raven and as his indentures date from 1876 it may be assumed that from joining the company in 1875 he was kept busy around the works doing whatever was required of him.

In addition, the 50th anniversary of the Stockton & Darlington Railway was celebrated in true Victorian fashion on the 27th/28th September, 1875. The Directors of the NER voted £5,000 towards the event and decreed that it should be held in Darlington. In return, Darlington council chipped in with £1,000 to cover the cost of decorations.

The *Darlington and Stockton Times* of 18th September, 1875 printed an article entitled 'The Railway Jubilee' and from then until the celebrations were over devoted page after page to the event. It went into great detail of every aspect, noting that the marquee erected for the banquet was 176 feet long, 80 feet wide, 20 feet high, lit by gas chandeliers and with accommodation for 1,000 guests, whose names were carefully listed adding that Messrs Gladstone and Disraeli were unable to attend. Catering was provided by King & Brymer of London and the extensive menu, covering seven courses, included oysters, truffles, pâté de fois gras, a baron of beef, roast chicken, ham, pigeons, lamb and much, much more.

Writing in the same newspaper on the 2nd October, 1875, a special reporter wrote as follows:

I don't know who is responsible for the drawing up of the toast list, but to whoever that duty was assigned he cannot be congratulated upon the remotest approach to success but rather commiserated on the completeness of his failure. To fancy that after a dinner supposed to commence at half-past six o'clock (but which really did not start until seven) sixteen toasts could be proposed and responded to, was to partake largely of the faith that removes mountains. At 10 o'clock little more that half the toasts had been honoured.

He continues:

The dinner was a good one, the marquee with its decorations and sumptuously laid tables was as pleasing to the eye as was the music of Dan Godfrey's band to the ear; but the speaking, which ought to have been a feature of the evening, if not of the day, was dreary. It was a dismal banquet even though it cost two guineas a head.

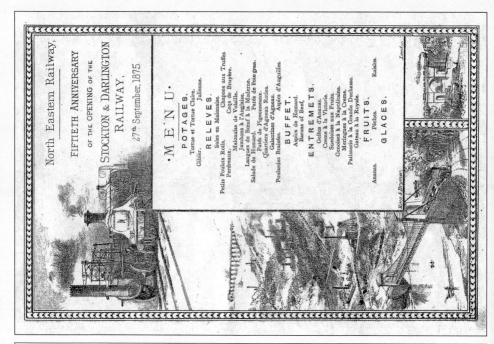

North Eastern Railway,

FIFTIETH ANNIVERSARY

OF THE OPENING OF THE

STOCKTON & DARLINGTON RAILWAY,

27th September, 1875

MENU.

POTAGES.
Tortue et Tortue Claire.
Gibier.   Julienne.

RELEVES.
Soles en Maïonaise.
Petits Poulets Rotis.   Chapons aux Truffes
Perdreaux.   Coq de Bruyère.
Maïonaise de Volaille.
Jambons à l'Anglaise.
Langues de Boeuf à la Moderne.
Salade de Homard.   Pâtés de Foiegras.
Pafés de Pigeonneaux.
Quartiers d'Agneau Roties.
Galantines d'Agneau.
Poulardes Braisées.   Aspics d'Anguilles.

BUFFET.
Aspics de Homard.
Barons de Beef.

ENTREMETS.
Gelbes d'Ananas.
Creme à la Victorie.
Sucdoises aux Fruits.
Genoises à la Napolitaine.
Meringues à la Creme.
Patisserie à la Grande Duchasse.
Gateau à la Royale.

FRUITS.
Ananas.   Pêches.   Raisins.

GLACES.

NORTH-EASTERN RAILWAY.

Special Train arrangements for Railway Anniversary at Darlington, on the 27th and 28th September, 1875.

MONDAY, SEPTEMBER 27th.

The 10 A.M. Scotch Express from King's Cross, timed to leave York at 2.35 P.M., will stop at Darlington for Passengers from South of York only.

Special Trains will run to Darlington as follows :—

From West Hartlepool at 10.25 A.M.   From Newcastle   at noon
„ Leeds   „ 10.30 A.M.   „ South Shields „   „
„ York   „ 11.0 A.M.   „ Sunderland   „ 12.15 P.M.

Note.—Invitation tickets will not be available by the South Express leaving Newcastle at 1.35 P.M.

In the evening, Special Trains will be run from Darlington as under, viz:—

Time.	Station from.	DESTINATION.
10 15 P.M.	Bank Top	Ripon, Harrogate, and Leeds.
10 30 „	Do.	Durham and Newcastle.
10 45 „	Do.	Sunderland and South Shields.
11 0 „	Do.	York and intermediate Stations.
11 15 „	Do.	Croft and Richmond Branch.
11 0 „	North Road	Shildon, Bishop Auckland, and Crook.
11 0 „	Do.	Preston Junction and Hartlepool.
11 15 „	Do.	Gainford, Barnard Castle, and Middleton-in-Teesdale
11 35 „	Do.	Stockton, Middlesbro', Guisbro', Redcar, and Saltburn.

TUESDAY, SEPTEMBER 28th.

Special Trains will run as under :—

Time.	Station from.	DESTINATION.
11 20 A.M.	Darlington, North Road	Stockton, Middlesbro', Redcar, & Saltburn.
1 30 P.M.	Middlesbro' Saltburn	Redcar and Saltburn.
3 45 „	Darlington,	Redcar, Middlesbro', Stockton, & Darlington.
9 30 „	North Road	Shildon and Bishop Auckland.

Guests, upon this occasion, can travel by the above, or by the ordinary trains announced in the Company's Time Bill.

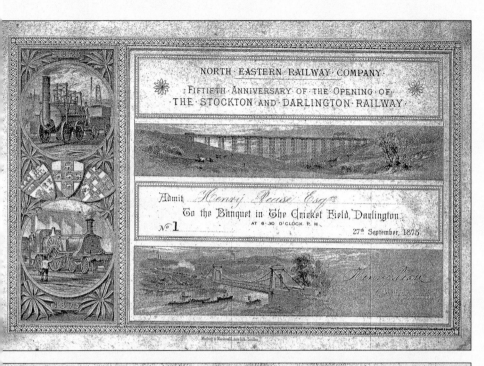

The reporter does not note at what time the banquet ended, but the NER ran late trains to Leeds, York, Sunderland, Newcastle, Middlesbrough and Saltburn serving intermediate stations.

With typical Victorian thoroughness, the deserving poor were not overlooked. The school children of Darlington were 'regaled with tea and a bun each in the large marquee'. It seems, however that they had to sing for their refreshments as the paper records that before tea they 'sang several of Moody and Sankey's hymns'.

The item continues, smugly:

> The inmates of the workhouse were not forgotten during this season of rejoicing. Through the liberality of Mr J.H. Bowman, the late Chairman of the Darlington Board of Guardians, the whole of the poor in the Workhouse were invited to tea on Monday afternoon. After partaking heartily of a substantial meal, tobacco and snuff were dispensed to those who used them.

Other features of the celebrations were the exhibition of locomotives at North Road works including a Stirling 'Single' from the Great Northern Railway and the variety of the decorations of houses and business premises, all carefully listed. For instance, Mr A. Heslop of Bondgate displayed 'a gas device representing a salmon' and Mrs Stephenson of the 'Hole in the Wall', Horesemarket displayed 'a star, five trophies of flags, windows decorated with scarlet cloth and fringe and rose trimmings'.

The highlight of the celebrations was the unveiling of the statue of Joseph Pease by the 4th Duke of Cleveland, preceded by a procession headed by 'six mounted Inspectors of Police' and immediately behind them the Band of the 13th Durham Rifle Volunteers followed by the Directors of the NER. The paper, leaving no stone unturned, listed the name of the individuals in the procession, the Friendly Societies with names of representatives and with a note of regret reported that:

> Although the brethren of the 'mystic tie' (Freemasons) could not take part in the public demonstrations at the Railway Jubilee, still they were not behindhand in celebrating the event according to their ancient custom.

Between 18th September, 1875 and 2nd October, 1875, the *Darlington and Stockton Times* devoted hundreds of column inches to the event, written in florid Victorian prose which was, here and there, patronizing.

The only sour note - apart from the criticism of the banquet - was that the inhabitants of Stockton-on-Tees felt marginalised. It was argued that since it was the Stockton and Darlington Railway that was being celebrated then Stockton should have had more of the action than it did. Neighbouring Middlesbrough felt much the same way although on Tuesday, 28th September, several of Middlesbrough's iron works were open to ticket holders.

And so the celebrations drew to a close with the presentation to the company of a portrait of Joseph Pease, a lengthy speech from T.E. Harrison, Chief Engineer, NER and a fireworks display. A good time was had by all, including, hopefully, young Vincent.

Chapter Two

Apprenticeship

It is difficult to imagine just how Raven reacted to Gateshead. His background was quintessentially Victorian middle class and no doubt his family, and father in particular, must have held high expectations of Raven and of his brother. Significantly, neither of them followed Raven senior, although Henry did go up to Cambridge where he read Law. It has not been possible to establish why Raven chose the NER but choose it he did and remained loyal to the company for the whole of his career. His life in Gateshead consisted of work and more work. Twelve hour days were the norm and the 16-year-old Vincent would have little time for socializing. In any case, in his early days at Gateshead it would take time for him to grasp not only the language with its dialect but also the culture. On the other hand, the austere regime of an English public school would no doubt have equipped him to cope. It may be assumed that he was in 'digs' and it is hoped that he had a kindly landlady who mothered him and helped through some difficult times. By the time that his apprenticeship proper commenced in 1876, the young Vincent would be familiar with the works and the environment.

The principle behind the pupil/apprentice system was that it was open to boys of 16/17 years, of a good educational background, with an interest in the industry, and, most importantly, whose parents could afford to pay the required premiums for five years. Some companies operated a two-tier system - pupilage and premium apprentice. The pupils were articled to the CME and the number of pupils that he was permitted to have was prescribed by his Directors. For instance during Raven's time as CME, he was allowed a maximum of five pupils per year each of whom paid £105 per year in return for which they had privileged status. The 'premiums' paid a nominal sum - usually £50 - for the privilege of working 53 hours per week for a weekly wage of 5s. in the first year increasing by 5s. per week plus overtime during each of the five years pupilage. The working week was reduced to 47 hours in 1918.

But all was not always sweetness and light in the world of pupils. This is best illustrated by quoting a rather plaintive memorandum from Wilson Worsdell headed 'Private' and dated 17th February, 1905. It is addressed to the Locomotive Committee.

It has been on my mind for two or three years past to bring to your notice the disability that I am under with regard to the Chief Mechanical Engineers of the principal English Railways and also the Chief Engineers of Permanent Way in connection with private pupils. As you are aware this is a uniform system on English Railways and it does seem unfair to myself that Mr Harrison, (Chief Engineer) Mr Cudworth (Civil Engineer) and Mr Newell (PW engineer) can all have private pupils and I have not at the same time the same privilege. Chief Mechanical Engineers on the other principal English Railways have the privilege of taking from six to eight pupils and I am informed that LB&SC [London, Brighton & South Coast Railway] small though it be, has just given its newly appointed Mechanical Engineer, Mr Marsh, liberty to take six private pupils.

Fletcher's '708' class 0-6-0 No. 724. Some 100 of these went into LNER ownership.

John Alsop Collection

Fletcher's '901' class 2-4-0 No. 363 at Tweedmouth.   *John Alsop Collection*

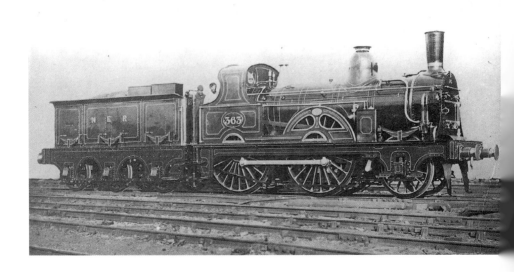

Apart from a personal question it must be of advantage to the Railway Company to have training up in the mechanical department of its service young men who have passed through the public schools and who after having had practical experience in our Locomotive Works would be good material from which we might select qualified men to take up responsible vacancies if need be.

As you may be aware I have frequently been asked if I have a vacancy for a private pupil, and of course my answer has always had to be in the negative.

The reply was sharp and to the point and came from the Locomotive & Stores Committee at its meeting held on 9th March, 1905:

Minute 5546 - A memorandum having been submitted from Mr Worsdell with reference to his being allowed to take private pupils, the Committee consent to his taking four pupils in the Company's shops who shall have passed a recognized qualifying examination.

Worsdell's anxiety was not altogether altruistic although his memorandum dwells on the advantages to the company. The fees from the pupils, or more accurately from their parents, were regarded as CME's 'perks' and although the pupils were articled to the CME, their training and supervision was invariably delegated to a senior member of the engineering staff. (When Raven was seconded to Woolwich Arsenal during World War I he was allowed to retain his pupil fees for the time that he was away, A.C. Stamer, the acting CME became responsible for the training but history does not reveal whether or not the fees were passed on.)

The premium apprentice was given a thorough training in every aspect of locomotive and carriage and wagon construction and operation from 12 hour shifts in the boiler shop to firing experience on the main line, whereas the 'ordinary' apprentice was bound to a specific craft - once a blacksmith always a blacksmith unless the individual was motivated to take advantage of what extra-mural courses were available. In this context, the Great Eastern Railway was at the forefront of education within the industry. There were six Directors' Scholarships tenable at East London College, but these lapsed at the Grouping and Gresley, not particularly interested, wanted to abolish the scholarships. He was prevailed upon by William Whitelaw - Chairman of the London & North Eastern Railway (LNER) - not to do so, although he - Gresley - restricted the number to six for the whole of the LNER.

The premium apprentices were on the fast track so far as promotion was concerned although there was no guarantee of employment with the company at the conclusion of training and many of them, having completed their apprenticeships, left the railway industry for pastures new. Two come to mind; W.O. Bentley who was apprenticed to H.G. Ivatt at Doncaster and Maurice Hall, Raven's last apprentice and who had a distinguished career in the steel industry. Others went on to hold high office within the country's railways; Raven and Peppercorn being two good examples. The latter joined the Great Northern as a premium apprentice under H.G. Ivatt, himself a premium apprentice, in 1905. He made steady progress through the ranks eventually succeeding Edward Thompson as CME of the LNER, taking the company into Nationalisation and oblivion. There are some interesting parallels in the lives

'708' class No. 712 was built in 1870 by Robert Stephenson & Co..

and careers of Raven and Peppercorn. Each was a child of the manse – Peppercorn's father was the Rector of Stoke Prior in Worcestershire; each went to public school – Peppercorn to Hereford Cathedral School; each was a pupil and each became CME of their respective companies.

In 1922 a group of former NER pupils decided to form an Association of Pupils and held the inaugural meeting at The County Hotel, Newcastle upon Tyne on 23rd February, 1922 at which it was unanimously agreed to invite Raven to become the first President and the letter of invitation was dated 4th April, 1922. Raven's reply, addressed to B.E. Harper, the first secretary of the Association was as follows:

> I duly received your letter of the 4th instant. As an old pupil myself I am very pleased indeed to know that you have decided to form an Association of North East Pupils. I think that it should have many interesting features and if kept up it will certainly be of increasing interest in years to come. I have very great pleasure in accepting the invitation to be President of the Association and shall hope to be present at one of your gatherings in order to welcome forward an inauguration of this kind.
>
> I shall have pleasure in giving you a list of the North Eastern Railway Pupils so far as I can trace them and this will be sent to you as soon as possible.

The Association's title was changed to the LNER Pupils' Association in 1936 and it lasted until the outbreak of World War II. The final officially recorded function was the 1939 Annual Dinner held in Newcastle. Between 1922 and 1939, the Association had 81 members, several of whom were senior officers within the railway industry - Arthur Peppercorn, Freddie Harrison, Cliffie Gold, R.A.Smeddle and G.F. Wintour amongst them and there were three presidents - Raven and A.C. Stamer under the NER 'banner' and Sir Nigel Gresley was the first and only President of the LNER Association. Reunion dinners were held regularly after the war but the trail goes cold after 1972.

But to return to education and railways. Although some of the universities offered courses in engineering in the late 19th century, they were few and far between. Cambridge was sufficiently enlightened to offer Mechanical Sciences and this was the route via which Edward Thompson entered the industry. As the 20th century progressed and university places in engineering became available, the demand for pupilages and premium apprenticeships dwindled. The outbreak of World War II cast a shadow on the system as it was assumed, initially, that the apprentices might be called for military service. It was, however, decreed, that railways were essential to the war effort and the apprentices were not called up. As far as can be ascertained, the scheme ended in 1946 and was replaced by an engineering apprenticeship scheme that not only required specific entrance qualifications but also day release at the local technical college.

As has been noted, the young Vincent was articled to Edward Fletcher, locomotive superintendent of the North Eastern Railway, in 1876. Fletcher was born in Northumberland in 1807, was apprenticed to George Stephenson in 1825 and from then on he was committed to the railways of the North East. Initially he was with the York, Newcastle and Berwick and when, in 1854 the North Eastern Railway was formed by the absorption of the York and North

'901' class 2-4-0 No. 926 at speed with a passenger train at Beningborough. No. 910 is preserved in the National Collection.

John Alsop Collection

Portrait of Edward Fletcher.   *LNER*

Midland and the Leeds Northern, Fletcher became locomotive superintendent of the newly formed company. His background was impeccable and his locomotives were highly regarded, especially the '901' class, considered by the *cognoscenti* as his masterpiece. One of the class, No. 910, is preserved and is in the National Collection. In *Locomotives of the North Eastern Railway* O.S. Nock waxes lyrical - 'stands old 910, in a splendour of brass work and gorgeous colouring that makes the Stirling eight footer, *Gladstone* and *City of Truro* look plain by comparison'.

The '901s' were built in batches between 1872 and 1882 eventually totalling 55 locomotives. The last five years of the decade coincided with Raven's apprenticeship and from 1878 to 1880 he was working in the drawing office. In the early part of his apprenticeship locomotives of the '708' class, introduced in 1870, were being turned out from Gateshead and from various contractors. They were rugged no-nonsense 0-6-0 tender engines, much loved by the men and the class eventually numbered 324. So rugged were the '708s' that, following various modifications, 100 of them passed into LNER ownership. Thus, Raven must have been involved with the development of two of Fletcher's most successful designs.

One of 'Ginx's Babies', 2-4-0 No. 1269. This class of six engines were originally built at Darlington in 1874 as 4-4-0s.

Chapter Three

Gateshead and Alexander McDonnell

Apprenticeship completed, Raven was appointed foreman at Gateshead works and district inspector responsible for the repair and maintenance of a stud of 200-plus locomotives that ranged in types from the '708' class to the 2-4-0 locomotives with 7 ft driving wheels, cylinders of 30 in. stroke and quaintly named 'Ginx's Babies'. The latter class was designed by William Bouch, brother of Thomas Bouch of Tay bridge fame and introduced in 1871/72. William, was locomotive engineer of the Stockton & Darlington Railway (S&DR) and remained in charge of locomotive affairs after the S&D became part of the North Eastern Railway. The 2-4-0s were troublesome from the start and it was not until Fletcher laid hold of them and rebuilt the entire class that they became useful secondary locomotives. In *Locomotives of the North Eastern Railway* O.S. Nock gives a brief account of the origin of the nickname. Ginx was the hero, or perhaps anti-hero, of a book by one Edward Jenkins MP. Ginx was appalled at the prospect of yet another addition to the family and threatened to drown the baby. He attempted to carry out his threat but the baby survived and Ginx jumped from the old Vauxhall Bridge and was drowned.

Despite the problems with the piston valves of the 'Ginx Babies' and his day-to-day responsibilities, Raven managed to have some social life for on 15th February, 1883 he married at St Stephen's Church, Low Elswick, Gifford Allan Crichton, the only daughter of John Walker Crichton, a Newcastle merchant. As the certificate shows, Raven senior performed the ceremony. The newly-married Ravens lived at Home Villa, Low Fell where their first child, Constance Gifford - Connie to the family - was born in 1883 followed by Edith Guendolen - Guen - in July 1884. Following the birth of Guen, Mrs Raven had a breather and Norman Vincent Crichton was born in April 1886, a third daughter, Annie, was born in July 1887 followed by a second son, Frederic Gifford, born in March 1889 by which time the Ravens had moved to Mardale Parade, Gateshead and had produced five children in six years.

Norman was sent to Uppingham where he was in School House and had an undistinguished career. Subsequently he worked for Mertz and McLellan. Constance married George Watson who was Clerk to the Justices at Darlington at St Cuthbert's Church, Darlington on 3rd November, 1910 and Guen married Edward Thompson at Holy Trinity Church on 25th June, 1913. The Watsons had two children, Michael who became a Squadron Leader and was killed in World War II and Mary who became Mrs Mary Iremonger. Little is known of Annie except that she was registered within three days of her birth and it is safe to conclude that she died in infancy. Frederic's name does not appear on the 1901 census return when he would have been 12 and was away at school, following which he worked for Indian State Railways and for sometime for Brazilian Railways returning to England to join the army. He was attached to the Railway Transport Section of the Royal Engineers and reached the rank of Captain. Unfortunately he died of wounds received on 18th March, 1917 and is buried in

McDonnell '38' class 4-4-0 No. 1500 at York.

Ste Marie Cemetery, Le Havre. Thus, the Ravens lost a son and a grandson as a result of two World Wars.

The easy-going Edward Fletcher retired in 1883 at the age of 76. He had been in office for 29 years and had made his mark on locomotive development. He was succeeded by Alexander McDonnell from the Great Southern & Western Railway of Ireland (GSWR). His CV was impeccable - an Honours Graduate of the University of Dublin he had wide ranging railway experience at home and abroad culminating in his appointment as locomotive superintendent of the GSWR at the age of 35. He was responsible for the re-organisation of Inchicore works, which in turn produced railway luminaries such as H.A. Ivatt, R.E.L. Maunsell and J.F. Aspinall.

McDonnell's arrival at Gateshead is described by O.S. Nock as that of 'a stranger in a strange land'. He was faced with a labour force that had confidence in the management and vice versa and that was happy with things as they were. He was also immediately responsible for some 1,500 locomotives as opposed to the few hundred that he left in Ireland and, as if to compound his difficulties, he followed Edward Fletcher, a much revered figure who was never too bothered about standardization or corporate images. He allowed the constituent companies to get on with what they did best and it is likely that on his retirement, the Directors of the NER decided that here was the opportunity for a 'shake-up' - their choice of a successor was, to say the least, unfortunate. Another appointment that was part of the re-organization was noted in minute 8798, 9th July, 1883: 'Resolved that Wilson Worsdell be appointed Assistant to the Locomotive Superintendent at a salary of £500 per annum with the tenancy, rent free, of the house formerly occupied by Edward Fletcher'.

The two years that followed were not happy for the NER and must have been miserable for McDonnell. He upset his labour force, he was lacking in tact and sensitivity and at the age of 53, he could be described as a middle-aged man in a hurry. He modified Fletcher's locomotives in ways in which the footplate men considered to be both unnecessary and retrograde - re-designing chimneys, introducing bogies and, crime of crimes, changing from right- to left-hand drive to mention but three examples. This change of drive was an obvious move as the signals and platforms were on the left-hand side of the track and placing the driver on the left-hand side of the footplate must have improved visibility. McDonnell set about standardization of locomotives and of working practices with something approaching missionary zeal and his presence in and around the works probably had the same effect on the men that the presence of Hamlet had on his stepfather. The constituent companies of the NER had continued to preserve their individual identities but in a period of 18 months McDonnell had introduced interchangeability of parts amongst the locomotives that he designed. Parallel with this he tightened up on discipline and in 1884 increased productivity by closing the old carriage works in Queen Street, York, and opening the new Holgate works. His gravest error, however, in the opinion of the enginemen, was the removal of the exhaust cocks from Fletcher's '901s'. Rebellion was in the air but he held his ground and the cocks had to go. Even then, he might have won the battle had it not been for the shortcomings of his locomotives. His class '38' 4-4-0s introduced in 1884 were inferior to Fletcher's '901s' - or did the footplate

McDonnell '59' class 0-6-0 No. 1487 near Low Fell, 18th August, 1913.

John Clewley Collection

Tennant '1463' class 2-4-0 No. 1506.

John Alsop Collection

Portrait of Alexander McDonnell.   *LNER*

crews not really try to get the best out of them? Eventually the class was removed from main line service and became extinct in February 1923.

McDonnell's class '59' 0-6-0 main line goods locomotives suffered a similar fate insofar as they met with wholesale opposition on the same grounds as did the 4-4-0s - no exhaust cocks, left-hand drive and so on. But enough was enough for McDonnell and in the autumn of 1884 he gave up the struggle and submitted his resignation, left the industry and, surprise, surprise his 0-6-0s were thereafter considered by many to be the best goods locomotives on the line.

Whilst the departure of McDonnell was inconvenient for the NER, the Board was relieved to see him go to the extent of paying him the balance of a year's salary plus £500 and no doubt considered that it got off lightly. His locomotives were inadequate and the situation could have become acute had not the General Manager, Henry Tennant, formed a committee consisting of the divisional locomotive superintendents with himself in the chair. So efficient was this committee that the first of the Darlington-built 'Tennants' were on the road before the last batch of McDonnell 4-4-0s were delivered by Hawthorn's.

It will not come as a surprise to learn that the Tennant 2-4-0s were received with something akin to rapture. After all had not sanity been restored? No bogies, the exhaust cocks were back and the locomotives were right-hand drive. Much of the credit must go to Wilson Worsdell who, as McDonnell's first assistant, must have been well aware of the turmoil that McDonnell caused and he, Worsdell, set about righting the wrongs. Here is a curious parallel with the retirement from the LNER of Edward Thompson some 60 years later. Arthur Peppercorn succeeded Thompson and under the influence of Bert Spencer *et al* produced the 'A1s' that incorporated all that was considered good 'Gresley Practice' (apart from the 2:1 valve gear) and the enginemen could be heard cheering from Top Shed to Ferryhill.

That Henry Tennant's action in forming his locomotive committee saved the day following McDonnell's hurried departure cannot be doubted. Tennant was appointed General Manager in 1871 and retired in 1891 but not before he had put locomotive affairs in good order. Twenty Tennant 2-4-0s - class '1463' - were built and the pioneer of the class, which was the last to be withdrawn, is preserved and is in the National Collection.

Portrait of T.W. Worsdell.   *LNER*

Portrait of Walter M. Smith.   *LNER*

Chapter Four

'TWW' and Compounding

Having successfully filled the void brought about by McDonnell's departure, Tennant lost no time in appointing a successor and in 1885 brought in T.W. Worsdell from the Great Eastern. 'TW' - as he was known - was an engineer of wide experience both at home and abroad and had learned the advantages of standardisation when working for the Pennsylvania Railroad at its Altoona works. On returning to the UK, he was appointed works manager at Crewe under F.W. Webb. He stayed at Crewe for 10 years, becoming involved with Webb's predilection for compounding before moving to the Great Eastern Railway. His appointment to the vacancy at Gateshead was something of a surprise as it was expected that Wilson Worsdell, TW's younger brother, who had had a similar career pattern would succeed.

What then was Raven doing during this upheaval? He continued in his job at Gateshead until 1883 - the year in which Fletcher retired - and he was involved in research on braking systems. Between 1872 and 1885 various types of brakes were tested amongst which were Tyrell, Clark and Webb, Sanders, Hardy and Herberlein, as used on Bavarian State Railways. Prior to 1872 locomotives only had handbrakes - trains had brake vans and the brakes were applied by the guard in response to whistle signals from the footplate.

A report submitted by Harrison and Drummond in 1879 strongly recommended the adoption of Westinghouse brakes. Subsequently, all NER passenger locomotives were so equipped and those used on East Coast Joint Stock (ECJS) trains were fitted additionally with vacuum ejectors as the GNR used vacuum brakes. Some ECJS coaches were dual braked but in 1911 reverted to vacuum only. There was a body of opinion amongst railway engineers that Westinghouse brakes should have been standard equipment on all British railways.

Apart from routine work, Raven distilled what he considered to be the best of McDonnell. There were certain aspects of McDonnell's work that Raven admired and that, as his career progressed, he introduced and that became standard practice. Thus, standardization and interchangeability of parts, organization of workshops and record keeping were part of the legacy left by the intransigent Irishman.

Compounding

Under Webb's influence T.W. Worsdell became an enthusiast for compound propulsion and in collaboration with August von Borries of Prussian State Railways TW developed a two-cylinder compound system which he introduced to the GER in 1884. Compound propulsion is based on the principal of using live steam twice - once at high pressure and then at low pressure. Thus, the high-pressure cylinder exhausts into the low-pressure cylinder. It was used successfully

A class 'C' 0-6-0 on a passenger turn near Arnside.

on marine and stationary steam engines - some were designed as triple expansion units in which steam was used three times - but was never fully exploited by the Country's railways although some companies persisted with it longer than did others. The London & North Western Railway (LNWR) under Webb, the Midland Railway under Deeley, Fowler and Johnson were protagonists of compound propulsion and, as noted above, the GER flirted with it under TW. This was not a howling success but nevertheless TW took his enthusiasm with him when he was translated to the NER. His first compound locomotive for the NER appeared in 1886. This was a two-cylinder 0-6-0 goods and was the precursor of the 'C' class of which there were eventually 171. From 1888 until his retirement in 1890, Gateshead turned out Worsdell - von Borries compounds in large numbers. Such was TW's enthusiasm that it spread to the continent. In a letter dated 31st May, 1889 M. Fassiaux, President of the International Railway Congress, requested details of TW's compound locomotives to be presented to the Congress at its meeting in Paris in July 1889. With unfailing courtesy, TW replied in detail. Brother Wilson, who succeeded TW, was no lover of compound propulsion with the exception of No. 1619 which was rebuilt as a three-cylinder Smith compound in 1898 along with the 4-4-2s referred to below.

Walter Mckersie Smith trained with the Midland Railway where his ideas on compound locomotives probably influenced S.W. Johnson. Before moving to the North Eastern, he was locomotive superintendent of Japanese State Railways. He was a gifted draughtsman, versatile and with a strong personality and not only did he persuade Wilson Worsdell to allow him to rebuild No. 1619 he also had a free hand in designing two 4-4-2s as four-cylinder compounds. No. 1619 - which took place in the trials arranged by Raven and Ramsay Kendal - was unusual in that the high pressure cylinder was inside and the low pressure cylinders were outside and that the high pressure and low pressure cylinders had separate cut-offs. C.J. Allen was of the opinion that it was the complexities of the separate cut-offs that decided Wilson Worsdell against further excursions into the world of compounding but it was in fact the results of the Raven/Kendal report and pressure from the Board that persuaded Worsdell. C.J. Allen refers to the 4-4-2 compounds as follows - '. . . the product (the 4-4-2 compounds) was probably the most advanced technically in the locomotive realm that the NER ever possessed'. Smith was a devotee of piston valves and in 1902 he presented a paper to the Institute of Mechanical Engineers on the subject of segmented valves of the type that he had designed and illustrated the advantages of piston valves over flat valves by quoting test results. He told the meeting that over a six-month period a class 'M1' 4-4-0 locomotive returned coal consumption figures of 29.55 lb. per mile whereas similar locomotives fitted with flat valves, the lowest figure was 32.33 and the average was 34.08 lb. per mile. Eventually, piston valves became standard on the NER. The fleet of NER compounds was rebuilt as simples but not before the Locomotive Committee ordered Worsdell to conduct comparative trials (Minute 2609, dated 5th October 1893). In advocating compound propulsion, TW had projected a saving of 12½ per cent in fuel costs. Unfortunately, he failed to deliver this saving and although the company persevered with compounds for some three years after his retirement, a note of alarm is discernable in the minutes of the Locomotive Committee. From minute 2772, 14th April, 1894:

'M1' class 4-4-0 No. 1629 pilots a down express as it leaves York in 1900.

John Alsop Collection

Compound engines . . . It then became doubtful whether the Compound Engines had effected the savings that had been expected . . . an apprehension that the high boiler pressure was going to increase the cost of maintaining them in working order . . . Two years further experience only confirmed the fears entertained by the Committee, but for their additional satisfaction the whole subject was referred to two competent engineers Messrs Raven and Kendal in the service of the company. They have presented a report and acting upon the recommendation it contains, the Locomotive Committee have decided not to resume the building of engines on the compound system.

The trials took place in October 1893 and Raven's diary entries show how thoroughly he and Ramsay Kendal prepared the ground.

Compound and non-compound Engines

13th October, 1893   Inspectors to be here this afternoon at my office.
Trains - Main Line Goods
Mineral trains
Engines to have same coal and an Inspector to ride on each engine.

14th October, 1893

Mr Hoy instructed to get out consumption of 10 compounds built 1887 to 1892.

Mr Stamer to be seen about getting out cost of repair etc.

Mr Horn (with Express link) to ride on Nos. 1619, 1620, 1621, 1622, 1623, 1624, 1625, 1626, 1627, and 1631.

Mr Rymer (South Main Line Goods) to ride on Nos. 606, 635, 625, 1299, 681, 107, 424, 1564, 1615 and 1563.

Mr Dent (Tyne Dock) to ride on Nos. 22, 86, 152, 667, 182, 1323, 1336, 1205, 1075 and 93. Similar work as near as possible.

Mr Birkett (South Express link) to ride on Nos. 1524, 1521, 1517, 1519, 1520, 1464, 1477, 1506, 1504 and 1472.

Mr Banks to see coal weighed on engines at Gateshead.

Trials begin Monday 16th.

To York from Newcastle with first Scotch engine No. 1459. Very heavy wind, steamed well and kept time. Engine priming a little.

Returned to York with 3.20 pm. No. 1524 Driver Dodds. Made up time. Engine ran very well. Cut-off did not sound very distinct and the blast pipe too did not seem exactly right. Very heavy wind.

17th October, 1893

Write to Mr Graham to put in 6 of the old class of engines on Tebay-Auckland.

22nd October, 1893

Engine No. 1323 compound would take only 30 instead of 35 out of No. 4 hole. Compounds are reduced to 30 empty – Tyne Dock. Martin says No. 480 a good strong engine, but compound better on road – stronger than ordinary engine. I saw engine No. 1513 start out of No. 3 hole with 29 on and van, but he stuck before getting up and had to set back.

24th October, 1893

Went to Sunderland and saw Mr Patterson who has two compounds running there and he says the drivers give them a very good name. Called at Monkwearmouth and saw Mr Wilkie, the yard foreman who says that although the compounds do not start so freely as the other engines and are not so handy in the yard, still he has nothing much to complain of. Tom Smith, foreman shunter, says the compound engines are slow at starting although they get well away on the road. However, he says the loads in Fletcher's time were heavier by 10 wagons than now, but their time was enough to enable them to do it. We also went to Blaydon and saw foreman shunter Greenlees who had nothing to complain of in the way the train engines shunt in the yard.

25th October, 1893

Went to Hartlepool and saw James, loco foreman, who says compound engines are not so strong as the others on a bank and in starting. He appears to prefer the old class.

Drivers' reports:

Adkinson	Poor driver, the only one who lost time.
Rainer	Compound goods do better than high pressure. No difficulty in shunting and starting
S. Tollerday	(Tyne Dock). No. 1512. Says he has no difficulty in starting, the only complaint is they do not lift more than 30 out of the holes. He uses about 25 pints of oil per 1,000. Is lighter on fuel than ordinary engine.

Rowland	Says he can take 35 easily.
E. Smith & E. Skipley	Corroborate above.
Stockton Yard	They say compound engines slower at shunting than others but I have never made any complaint. They take 10 to 15 minutes longer in shunting. I have heard it said they make it up again on the road.

John Medley of South Goods Yard says he has no complaints, about compounds unless they have a load of 36 wagons.
We went to Ferryhill and saw loco foreman Sheppard. He has no compounds under his charge but he has noticed they do not get away with a load so well as other engines. They are slower in shunting but appear to run well when they get away with a train.

27th October 1893 York
Saw Houseman foreman shunter. He says compounds in making up load would take ½ hour to ordinary engine's 20-25 minutes. Foreman Clark says compounds not safe. Considers some men better than others with them.

Shaw	Compounds now do their shunting very much better than they used to owing to the men being more used to them.
Bates	(Assistant to Steel) Says he had trouble with steam pipe joints.
Steel	No special case against compounds but he has heard they are slow at shunting and bad with stopping.

Following the trials the Raven/Kendal report was submitted to Lowthian Bell, Chairman of the Locomotive Committee. It was comprehensive and even-handed and ended with the comment:

The compound engines are alright once fairly away with a load in ordinary circumstances, but for shunting or starting very much inferior to the ordinary engines. Drivers generally prefer compounds for through goods traffic but consider them unhandy and slow for other purposes. Those in charge of mineral traffic inform us that the simple engine for their purposes is much to be preferred.

The report, complete with performance tables and consisting of 20 pages, 15 in. x 10 in. is signed by Raven and Kendal and endorsed, not exactly in ringing tones, by Worsdell. And that, effectively, was the end of compound propulsion on the NER and TW's compounds were re-built as simples. Along with compounding went Joy's valve gear and in came Stephenson's link motion and piston valves. Following the formation of the London & North Eastern Railway Gresley toyed with compounding in the form of his four-cylinder watertube-boilered 4-6-4 locomotive but even he had to admit defeat and finally gave up in 1937. After two years in the wilderness at Darlington works and - insult of insults - being used as a stationary boiler, the locomotive was rebuilt as a three-cylinder simple with a Stephenson boiler and streamlining identical with Gresley's 'A4s'. It did, however, have the distinction of being the last compound locomotive built for any British railway.

Chapter Five

Promotion and Darlington

T.W. Worsdell retired in 1890 and he was succeeded by his brother, Wilson. T.W. had made a strong impression on North Eastern locomotive practice and given the locomotives a family likeness - flared chimneys, combined splashers and a large two-windowed cab amongst other details. He was concerned with the comfort of the footplate crews and his commodious cabs afforded protection for driver and fireman in the harsh winters for which the North East is renowned. Wilson Worsdell was a worthy successor. He had spent several years with the LNWR and joined the NER at Gateshead in 1883. Raven was appointed assistant divisional locomotive superintendent for the northern division in 1888 and he continued in that office under Wilson Worsdell until 1893 when he was appointed chief assistant locomotive superintendent.

Minute 10246: Mr Graham (divisional superintendent, Darlington) asked to be relieved owing to ill-health and Mr Worsdell recommends Mr Raven to be removed from Gateshead to Darlington as Chief Assistant. Age 36 [actually he was 34] served 20 years. Present salary £286 - to be £450, as Locomotive Running Superintendent.

(Signed) J.D. Dent, Chairman

and so in accordance with the Board's wishes the Raven family headed for Darlington. Further promotion followed and in 1895 at the early age of 36 - by which time had served under four CMEs (five if Tennant is included), he became assistant mechanical engineer. With a growing family to support the promotion, with its increase in salary, must have been most welcome. The 1901 census shows that the family home was Alpine Cottage, 32 Whessoe Street and the household consisted of Raven, Mrs Raven, Constance, Guen plus Alice Fawcett, cook, Isabel Smith, nurse and Annie Inglis, servant. Norman was at Uppingham and Frederic was at The Mount School, Northallerton. There is no reference to Annie. Connie and Guen were educated privately at Polam School, a Quaker foundation school in Darlington. Connie left Polam in 1902 and in the Spring of 1903 she went to Evendine, a finishing school at Colwall near Malvern. Here she obtained certificates in dressmaking and housework and was so highly regarded that having completed her year she was asked to stay on to cover for a member of staff who was on long term absence.

On her return to Darlington and along with Guen, Connie became involved with Polam School Old Scholars' Association. Each was very active, Connie becoming secretary in 1906 and in 1907 Guen proposed that £1 should be given for a golf prize. In the same year Connie was responsible for the presentation of a silver tea and coffee service to the Headmistress, Miss Bayes, on the occasion of her wedding. In 1909 Connie played in the tennis match between past and present students. Thereafter, both Connie and Guen seem to have become disenchanted with the poor response to the sports events at Re-Unions, Connie averring that many OS were 'too modest'.

The four years between 1898 and 1902 saw a rapid expansion of Darlington works to the extent that capacity was almost doubled. £120,000 was invested and productivity increased with the introduction of electrically-operated cranes in 1900. For example, before the installation of overhead electric cranes, it took 20 men 330 minutes to remove the pony truck from a locomotive - following the installation it took four men 12 minutes.

It is highly likely that this early use of electricity alerted Raven to its possibilities and, according to R.A.S. Hennessey, he went to the USA 'as an acolyte of electrification and returned a high priest'.

The year 1902 was a significant one for Raven. Apart from his involvement with the up-dating of the machinery both in Darlington works and Middlesbrough Dock and his visit to the USA, he received further promotion. The Locomotive and Stores Committee under minute 4944, dated 30th January, 1902 approved the promotion of Raven to chief assistant mechanical engineer at a salary of £1,400 pa. At the same time, Stamer's salary was increased to £400 pa and technical assistant Charlie Baister's to £450 pa.

Raven's progress coincided with the retirement in 1891 of Henry Tennant and the appointment of George Stegmann Gibb as his successor as General Manager. Thus, with Wilson Worsdell in charge of locomotive affairs and the dynamic Gibb in post there was something akin to a palace revolution in the halls of the NER. Gibb, a Scotsman by birth, was appointed solicitor to the company in 1882. He was very much an organization and methods man and on his elevation to the General Manager's post he set about re-organizing the administration. He was forward-looking and was very much in the forefront of the recruitment of young graduates who formed the basis of his traffic apprentice scheme. Two of Gibb's recruits were R.L. Wedgwood, who was divisional goods manager at

Portrait of Wilson Worsdell.   *LNER*   Portrait of George Stegmann Gibb. *LNER*

Newcastle in 1905, promoted to chief goods manager in 1912 and in 1922 appointed Chief General Manager of the LNER (Sir Ralph's daughter, Dame Veronica Wedgwood, was only the third woman to be awarded the Order of Merit since its inception in 1902) and Eric Geddes, later Sir Eric, who joined the NER in 1904 - by 1911 he was Deputy General Manager. His approach to business methods and his dynamic personality endeared him to Lloyd George as a result of which Geddes's rise to stardom was meteoric. He was, in turn, Deputy Director General of Munitions, Inspector-General of Transportation, First Lord of the Admiralty, MP for Cambridge and he held, simultaneously for some months, the ranks of Major-General and Vice-Admiral. He masterminded the grouping of the railways into the 'Big Four' and Geddes it was who insisted on the letters 'NER' being incorporated into the new company's title but he is best remembered for his expenditure cuts in the civil service in 1922, known colloquially as the 'Geddes Axe'.

Raven was acknowledged as a very good administrator and his appointment in 1893 brought with it responsibility for disciplinary matters. Subsequent events in his career, however, indicate that personnel affairs were not Raven's strong suit. The following extracts from his diaries underline the point:

6th August, 1894
Webster, a driver who was discharged some 28 months ago through his daughter writing an anonymous letter, called to see if I could do anything for him. I did not see him as I sent out word it would be useless as I could not interfere in this case.
Driver Williamson (Shildon) called re his fine of 5s. for allowing a shunter to ride on his engine. I would not entertain the return of his fine.
Yeates, works labourer wants a boilersmith's place. I told him I should have to give any vacancy to those who had recently left here.

8th October, 1894
Thomas Crowe came to see me concerning suspension and I pointed out to him what a serious offence it was going on a single line without a staff.

The following entries reveal Raven's concern with costs and economies:

18th November, 1894
Engines ordered out and returned without being used. Mineral mileage in the north so much less than in central per hour. Engine power in the north wasted. Suggestions as to amendment. Hartlepool engines returned to shed without making a full day and this causes time to be paid for nothing.

24th November, 1894
Edinburgh working. I am getting out the difference in the cost of engines working between Newcastle and Edinburgh and Newcastle and Berwick. The only saving seems to be the difference in the coal and stores used, with the extra repairs and shed staff at Edinburgh. If all engines are taken to Edinburgh the difference in repair cannot be great. We lose engine mileage of 115 per day.

5th January, 1895
J. Burnard (Shildon) came to see me about having another test, he being very bad in colour. I refused.

T.W. Worsdell 'F' class 4-4-0 No. 1537 with safety valves blowing.

25th January, 1895
Driver Potts came to see me, he being under suspension having been reported under influence of drink. Told him he would have to remain off until enquired into.

25th January, 1895
Mrs Jackson, Bank Top, came to see me concerning her husband, labourer, in prison for debt. I consider him as left - said that he could see me when he come [*sic*] out - I have filled the place up in the meantime.

2nd March, 1895
W.M. Lax cleaner Middlesbrough having had complaints from Mr Cornish concerning him. I have told him unless he does better and I hear no future complaints he will have to go.

5th March, 1895
Driver Potts who has been discharged for drink came to see me asking if no sort of job can be given him. I said I could do nothing as the matter was in Mr Wordsell's hands.

5th March, 1895
W. Pindar - engine driver York - sent for this man owing to the unsatisfactory character given of him by Mr Bailey. He (Pindar) is a man of 64 and he says that he has never tasted drink for 13 months and has been troubled by rheumatism and I told him to let Bailey know in future if he was ill & to try to keep better time and not let me hear of him again.

19th March, 1895
C. Modran, cleaner (Gateshead) discharged for being on the footplate of an engine. If Mr Bennett is agreeable to having him back I should have no objection.

In August 1895 the second Great Rail Race to the North from London to Aberdeen was at its zenith. The event and the circumstances leading up to this somewhat juvenile example of railway operation have been written about to the point of tedium. Suffice it to say that Raven as assistant locomotive superintendent, NER, was involved to the extent that he was a member of the committee that met on 12th August, 1895 and that decided the schedule for the period 19th-23rd August. It was agreed that the 8 pm King's Cross-Aberdeen was to arrive at 5.40 am, 20 minutes earlier than the equivalent West Coast train. He rode on the footplate of No. 1621, a T.W. Worsdell 'F' class locomotive with driver Turner at the regulator from York to Edinburgh. Turner was, by all accounts, a Victorian equivalent to Bill Hoole and Ted Hailstone* and was keen to create a record run to Edinburgh. The press took an interest in the 'race' and had representatives on the train and the outcome of the event was that the average speed between London and Edinburgh was increased.

---

* Bill Hoole and Ted Hailstone were top link drivers at Top Shed in the 1950s. They were, amongst the platform-enders at King's Cross, legends in their own time, a reputation they were happy to promote. In the days of one engine/one crew, Hoole had 'A4' class 4-6-2 *Sir Nigel Gresley* and Hailstone had 'A4' *Silver Link*. Each was known as a speed merchant: neither was a particularly outstanding driver.

Chapter Six

USA and Electrification

Despite the failure of the NER's bankers - J. & J.W. Pease - in August 1902 (an event that eventually cost the company £125,000) accompanied by H.A. Watson and W.J. Cudworth, Raven was sent to the USA where the party arrived on 15th October, 1902. Thanks to the prudence of the Directors in having a contingency fund, the visit that was planned before the 'crash' went ahead. The brief was to see as much of American practice as possible in a month. The three of them certainly covered some ground and, of course, produced a report on their return. The following extracts illustrate how some of what was seen impressed and, to a lesser extent, influenced Raven:

Discipline

'In the lower grades they (American railways) are much more ready to dismiss than we are. By changing men often the Unions do not get so strong. For instance, a permanent way ganger has full power of dismissal and so long as he gets the work done, his superiors do not ask by whom'. The report makes reference to the facilities at stations and concedes that they are superior to those in UK.

Office facilities

The extensive use of the telephone was commented upon and it was appreciated that time and money could be saved if more use was made of the 'phone and if the NER offices were 'open plan' (the term wasn't used). Also noted were the facilities provided for the staff - 'provision of lavatories, conveniences and feeding facilities' (one cannot help but wonder just how NER employees fared without the foregoing).

Locomotives

The team was impressed with the following features: steel fireboxes with iron stays; much less time spent on maintenance than in UK; very little painting (of locomotives); no splashers; all working parts accessible.

Electrification

'All that we have seen and heard shew [*sic*] that we are right in what we are doing and that Mr Mertz has advised us well.' (Charles Mertz and Raven were close friends - did this influence the final sentence?)

Electrification and the NER

The NER was pressured into adopting electric traction as a result of an electric tramway that was constructed around Newcastle in 1901. The Directors of the NER, alarmed at the effect that the tramway was having on the company's receipts - approximately four million passenger miles lost in a year - decided to authorize the electrification of 37 route miles of track. The lines were from Newcastle Central to North Shields and Tynemouth; from Tynemouth to Monkseaton via Cullercoats and Whitley Bay; from Monkseaton back to Newcastle via Backworth. The third rail system was used operating at 600 volts DC and was opened in stages between March and July 1904. There was a mile long branch from Trafalgar Yard to Quayside Yard that involved a ruling gradient of 1 in 27 and a tunnel. For reasons of safety, overhead supply was provided in the tunnel. Two locomotives provided the motive power and were numbered 1 and 2. They were of the Bo-Bo wheel arrangement with BTH traction equipment and Brush bogies. At the end of August 1903 13 cars were built and, in the middle of September, the first completed train was inspected by Worsdell, Raven, Stegmann Gibb and the Directors at the old York station. The train did a series of steam-hauled runs in the York area before heading for Heaton and its first electrically-hauled working on 27th September, 1903. Early in 1904 Chas H. Mertz, the consulting engineer to the NER Tyneside electrification project, delivered a paper to the British Association at its meeting in Cambridge in the course of which he trumpeted the virtues of electricity in general and for traction in particular. At about the same time, G.F. Groves, the chief draughtsman, carriage & wagon, pointed out to Raven that the carriages built for the North Tyneside project were not up to standard and had been bodged. Bodged or not, the system began operating on 29th March, 1904.

The experience that Raven gained with the North Tyneside scheme not only fired his enthusiasm but also spurred him on. In 1911 the General Manager A. Kaye Butterworth raised the question of further electrification and as a result Raven again visited the USA accompanied by his deputy A.C. Stamer and a rising young Cambridge graduate engineer, Edward Thompson, and returned brimming with ideas. He lost no time in submitting a report, dated 12th January, 1912, and his estimated price for electrification was £1.5 million.

In a memorandum to Raven dated 8th August, 1912, Butterworth pointed out that Raven's estimate was higher than he - Butterworth - expected and suggested that any necessary information could be obtained from existing systems. This did not go down well with Raven and eventually a compromise was reached and Butterworth, with a certain show of reluctance, accepted the electrification of the Shildon to Erimus Yard line, 18½ route miles, 50 track miles. Butterworth derived some comfort from the fact that the route chosen was mineral only and did not have tunnels or complicated junctions. Thus any problems and/or unforeseen difficulties would cause the minimum of inconvenience and disruption. Whether or not the Board realised that by approving the Shildon-Erimus Yard electrification scheme it was setting a precedent in Great Britain is not known but approval was given in 1913.

The yard at Shildon was a collecting point for the output of the West Durham coalfield, and Erimus Yard, opened in 1908, was a distribution point for coal

Bo-Bo shunting locomotive built in 1904 photographed at South Gosforth in April 1964.

John Clewley

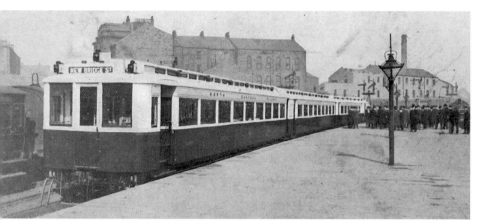

A commercial postcard showing the first electric train from Newcastle to Benton on 29th March, 1904.

John Alsop Collection

A veiw inside the first Newcastle to Benton electric train, 29th March, 1904.

John Alsop Collection

An electric set passes through Backworth station.   *John Alsop Collection*

An electric unit awaits departure at Tynemouth.   *John Alsop Collection*

Portrait of Alexander Kaye Butterworth.   *LNER*

and other materials for shipment and for the heavy industry of Tees-side. (Erimus yard derives its name from Erimus which is the motto on the Coat of Arms of Middlesbrough. The translation of Erimus is 'We shall be' - somewhat unfortunate in the light of subsequent events.)

Raven's plans for the electrification programme included 1.5 kv overhead supply and 10 locomotives to be built at Darlington to his design. The scheme was implemented and going ahead when war was declared in August 1914 at which time the NER was at the height of its powers. The Directors were not put off, in spite of the war and in spite of the fact that the company was moving into the unknown - there were no precedents for heavy freight electric locomotives such as were built at North Road works to Raven's designs. The work continued and the first section of the line from Shildon to Bowesfield Junction was commissioned on 1st August, 1915 and the remainder to Erimus Yard was commissioned on 1st January, 1916, by which time Raven had been with the Ministry of Munitions at Woolwich for some months (*see Chapter Nine*). One wonders whether or not Raven was present at the commissioning - perhaps it was left to his able lieutenant, A.C. Stamer.

The motive power fleet consisted of 10 x 1,100 hp Bo-Bo locomotives. They proved to be more than equal to the task for which they were designed - one of them hauled a train of 92 empties - about 800 tons - on a test run and maintained an average speed of 23 mph. On 14th February, 1913, the NER entered into an agreement with the Newcastle-upon-Tyne Electric Supply Company, the Cleveland and Durham County Electric Power Company and Cleveland and Durham Electric Power Company for the power supply. The conditions were that the NER was to lay the cables between the supplying companies' mains and the sub-stations. There were two sub-stations, one at Aycliffe and the second at Erimus Yard. The former had three phase, 40 cycle, 20 Kv supply: the latter 11 Kv supply. Rotary converters reduced the voltage to 1.5 Kv. Overhead equipment was supplied by Siemens, sub-station equipment by BTH,

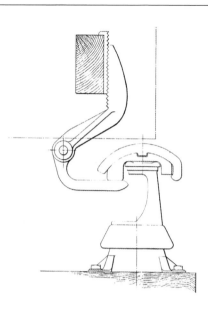

GENERAL ARRANGEMENT OF PROTECTED CONDUCTOR RAIL

SCALE

Sketch Nº 36·32/8·131

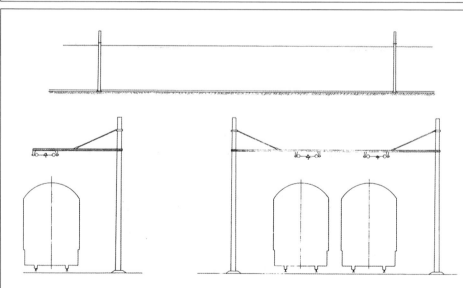

North Eastern Railway.

General Arrangement of Siding Track Construction. Type B.

Scale: ⅛" = 1ft.

Sketch Nº 363/8 28

Frames and wheels of electric locomotive No. 9.

Doug Hardy

Electric locomotive No. 9 hauled by a Worsdell 0-6-0T at the 1925 Centenary procession.

Doug Hardy

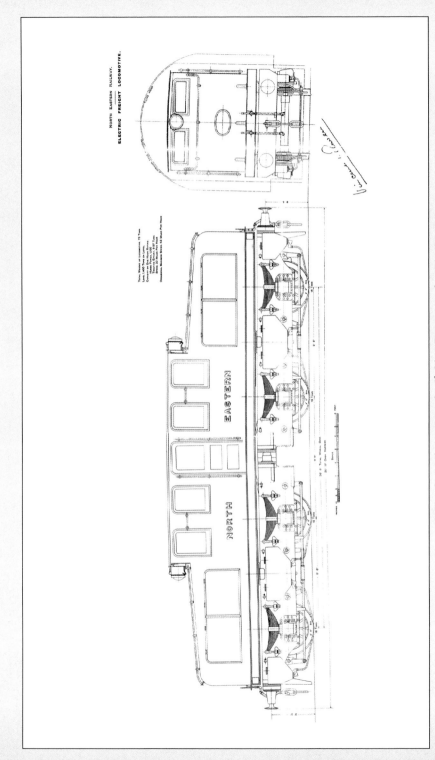

NORTH EASTERN RAILWAY.

ELECTRIC FREIGHT LOCOMOTIVE.

Bo–Bo electric locomotive for Shildon–Erimus yard services.

switchgear by Reyrolle and the contractors to operate and maintain it. In addition, the Newcastle-upon-Tyne Electric Supply Company agreed to give priority for supply to the NER. In service, the locomotives regularly handled trains of 1,400 tons to Erimus Yard with 800 tons of empties on the return leg to Shildon and they put in four trips per day until a gradual decline in traffic between the wars and the need to renew the infrastructure made it uneconomic to continue with electric traction. The locomotives were never fully utilised, were withdrawn *en bloc* on 8th July, 1935 and stored at Darlington and Gosforth, the catenaries were removed and the line reverted to steam working.

The Shildon-Middlesbrough scheme was successful within the limitations of (a) the overhead system that supplied the energy to the locomotives and (b) the continuing economic viability of the Durham coalfield. By 1935 both factors were in doubt. Since the line relied heavily on movement of coal, the LNER decided against further investment and the supply lines were dismantled. Of course, 1935 was a bad year for anything that wasn't steam-hauled on the LNER. How could an historically interesting line that was in need of attention compare in importance with 'Silver Link' *et al*? The electric locomotives that Raven had introduced had given 20 years' trouble free service on the system and were a significant step in the direction that eventually led to the electrification of the East and West Coast main lines some 35/45 years later.

Various suggestions were mooted for the future of the locomotives, one of which was to transfer them to the Worsbrough branch line. This steeply graded mineral-only line constructed by the Great Central Railway (GCR) originated in Wath Yard in South Yorkshire, skirted Barnsley and joined the Sheffield-Manchester line at Silkstone West Junction. Electrification of the line was begun in 1938 and much of the foundation work and some of the overhead steel work was in place when World War II was declared. The project was immediately shelved, was not recommenced until 1947 and by the time that the work was completed, the NER locomotives had been in store some 12 years. Nothing came of the idea of sending them to Worsbrough although one of them - BR No. 26510 - was sent to Ilford as the depot shunter in August 1949. In 1960 there was a change of voltage on the Liverpool Street suburban lines rendering No. 26510 redundant. It languished at Goodmayes until April 1964 when it was returned to Doncaster for scrapping.

Back from the Ministry, Raven was delighted with the progress made with the Shildon line. Teething problems had been overcome and he was quickly promoting further electrification - this time for passenger traffic from Newcastle to York with plans to electrify from Northallerton to Newport Yard via Eaglescliffe and from Ferryhill to Middlesbrough via Stockton. The reasoning behind this was that was there was much goods and freight traffic into and out of Tees-side. Accompanied by Frank Lydall from Messrs Mertz & McLellan, Sir Vincent - as he now was - visited eight railways in the USA and submitted a 72 page report that contained outline drawings of two proposed electric locomotives and included the following deathless paragraph:

> In all the visits to electrified railways and in all the discussions with railway officials and engineers, the various technical and financial questions relating to the North Eastern Railway were constantly borne in mind. The information received fully justified the

Bo-Bo electric locomotive No. 3 in the paint shop yard at Darlington.

various assumptions which formed the basis of the Chief Mechanical Engineer's report of October 1918 and support the various views expressed therein as to the individual advantages inherent in electric operation.

An *ad hoc* committee was appointed to consider further electrification based on the report.

The report submitted by Raven and C.F. Bengough (Chief Engineer) contains closely reasoned and cogent arguments in favour of electrification of the main line from York to Newcastle, arguments supported by facts and figures. The report emphasises the experience gained in operating the Shildon-Newport line:

> Regular working with these locomotives started in July 1916 and since that date nearly all the traffic has been worked by them. The experiment has proved eminently satisfactory and the experience thus gained in heavy electric traction is invaluable. [It continues, almost dismissively:] Slight troubles have, of course, been experienced. With the overhead equipment it was found that at some exposed parts of the line the heavy gales caused the wires to sway and foul the bow on the locomotive, but this has been cured by placing additional supports to the wires thus reducing the span and making the wire more rigid.

The conclusions arrived at from the figures are, to say the least, questionable. The report states:

> We have endeavoured to compare as accurately as possible the cost of working the Shildon - Erimus line by steam and by electric locomotives. The comparison has not been an easy one owing to the fact that the only steam figures that we have for this portion of the line are 1913 and the cost of wages and materials have altered to a large extent since that date. We have, however, *added a percentage to these figures in order to bring them to 1918 proportions* [author's italics]. The number of locomotives in use was five whereas in order to perform the same work, with steam we should have had to make the use of 13. [The report continues, enthusiastically:] We have been encouraged by these results to consider an extension of electrification and have chosen for this purpose the Main Line from York to Newcastle with its principal intermediate feeders, Stockton to Ferryhill and Stockton to Northallerton.

It was proposed that at the southern end electrification would end (or begin) at Dringhouses signal box and at the northern extremity it would terminate at Newcastle Central where it would link up with the existing Tyneside lines. Eastwards, it was proposed that the terminating point would be Erimus Yard, the new lines linking with the Shildon-Newport electrified lines at Bowesfield Junction and at Stillington Junction.

As might be expected, the report goes to great lengths to state the advantages of electric traction over steam, advantages that are now regarded at obvious. Included in the comprehensive list are: saving of labour on shed - boilerwashers, glandpackers, ashpit men, brick arch men (to mention but a few) are not required.

Better use of locomotives: 'It takes two to three hours to light up and raise steam in a steam locomotive but an electric locomotive is ready for work at a moment's notice'.

On the road: 'A large amount of unproductive time is incurred with a steam locomotive in taking water, fire cleaning and turning. These are not incurred with the Electric' [*sic*].

Effects of the weather: 'In very cold weather the electric locomotive has another advantage in that it is not subject to the effects of radiation and freezing as is the steam engine while in hot weather the dangers of starting fires in the dry vegetation alongside the track by cinders falling from the engine is non-existent'.

Compensation to trackside land owners: 'The cost of compensation to owners located along the route of a railway in this country is considerable due to fires, caused by hot ashes discharged from the uptake of a steam locomotive is considerable, particularly during a period of drought . . .'

Also included are timekeeping, damage to rolling stock and better use of wagon stock.

The report goes on to reinforce its arguments with appendices and tables some of which are produced herewith.

Steam		*Electric*	
Ton Miles	4,577,299	Ton Miles	3,800,284
	Per 100 ton miles (d.)		*Per 100 ton miles (d.)*
Coal and Water	4.781	Electric Energy	3.121
Stores	0.278	Stores	0.159
Enginemen's Wages and Running Shed Expenses	3.810	Enginemen's Wages and Running Shed Expenses	1.496
Guards' Wages	1.103	Guards' Wages	0.568
		Train Preparers	0.121
Maintenance of Telegraph and Telephones	0.089	Maintenance of Telegraph and Telephones	0.144
Repairs and Renewals of Locomotives	4.754	Repairs and Renewals of Locomotives	1.171
		Repairs and Renewals of Overhead Equipment	4.149
Total	*14.815*	*Total*	*10.929*

Statement shewing steam and electric engines
necessary to work passenger and freight service over the sections
York-Newcastle via Team Valley and Northallerton-Ferryhill via Stockton

		Steam			Electric	
Passenger Service	*In steam*	*Spare 33%*	*Total*	*At Work*	*Spare 25%*	*Total*
Newcastle	20	6	26	9	2	11
Durham	2	1	3	2	1	3
Ferryhill	1	-	1	1	-	1
Middlesbrough	1	-	1	1	-	1
Darlington	4	2	6	4	1	5
York	13	4	17	6	2	8
TOTAL	41	13	54	23	6	29

Freight Service	In steam	Steam Spare 33%	Total	At Work	Electric Spare 25%	Total
Newcastle	23	8	31	12	3	15
Ferryhill	7	2	9	4	1	5
West Hartlepool	3	1	4	-	-	-
Stockton	10	3	13	8	2	10
Newport	32	11	43	17	5	22
Darlington	17	6	23	11	2	13
Thirsk	5	2	7	3	1	4
York	18	6	24	9	2	11
Normanton	1	-	1	-	-	-
Total	116	39	155	64	16	80
Grand total	157	52	209	87	22	109

Summary
Annual cost (£)

	Steam	Electric	Saving
Wages	197,997	144,800	53,197
Coal and Water	241,963		10,122
Electric Energy	-	231,841	
Stores	22,253	11,908	10,345
Repairs and Renewals	177,485	69,554	107,931
Depreciation	19,167	14,294	4,873
Total	658,865	472,397	186,468

Annual Saving			£186,468
Deduct Engineers Maintenance (see Appendix Six)		£65,443	
Net Annual Saving			£121,025

From the minutes of the NER, minute 12181, dated 25th July, 1919:

The General Manager [A. Kaye Butterworth] submitted a report on a proposal [from VLR] to electrify the main line from York to Newcastle. It was agreed that a committee should be appointed as under: Mr Pease: Sir Hugh Bell: Captain Kitson: Mr Lupton signed - Knaresborough, Chmn

From the minutes - 12187, dated 19th September, 1919:

The committee have examined the proposals and have satisfied themselves in view of the fact that there are considerable arrears of engine maintenance to be made good and that electric working would enable the traffic to be worked by a much smaller number of locomotives, the substitution of electric for steam power could be carried out at a figure which would justify the initial outlay provided agreement could be made for a supply of current.

Resolved that the scheme be approved and submitted to the Minister of Transport.

Signed - Knaresborough - Chmn

From the minutes - 12207, dated 9th January, 1920:

The General Manager reported he had received a letter from the Minister of Transport that the Minister approved in principle the proposal to electrify the main line and the immediate construction of electric locomotives. The Minister was of the opinion that the time had come when an attempt should be made to obtain more uniformity of type.

Signed - Knaresborough – Chmn

From the minutes - 12238, dated 11th June, 1920:

The Government would not be willing to assist in raising money for electrification.

Signed - Knaresborough - Chmn

From the minutes - minute 12278 dated 10th December, 1920:

The Chief Mechanical Engineer reported on his visit to the United States. Suggestions in the report are that:
(1) an electric locomotive of the gearless design should be constructed.
(2) The main line from Darlington to Newcastle is electrified.
Resolved that the matter be referred to the committee appointed on 25th July, 1919.

In spite of the fact that Government money was not forthcoming, the scheme went ahead and in 1922 the prototype 2-Co-2 locomotive was built at Darlington to the designs of a team made up of Raven, Mertz and Lydall with the ultimate responsibility resting with Raven. It was fitted with Metro-Vick electrical equipment, overhead collection, dual braking and steam heating. Mertz and McLellan's 'man on the job' at Darlington was none other than Norman Raven, the CME's son. Britain's first electric express locomotive was of the 2-Co-2 type and was allocated number 13 - in view of its subsequent history this might have been an augury.

No. 13's most striking feature is generally accepted to have been its 6 ft 8 in. driving wheels and R.A.S. Hennessy in his *The Electric Railway That Never Was* states: 'Those who remember No. 13 operating under power still wax enthusiastic on the subject. On starting, the giant helical springs which pressed on the spokes would suddenly compress. Then she would move away with startling acceleration: thrilling, occult and swift'.

It was intended that No. 13 should be capable of 65 mph hauling a 450 ton train, with a maximum speed of 90 mph. On completion it had trials with the dynamometer car on the Shildon-Erimus line as this was the only source of 1.5 Kv DC supply. Metropolitan Vickers published performance figures as part of a publicity campaign:

Main line electric locomotive: actual test results. This locomotive which is intended for hauling East Coast Main Line trains over the electrified portion of the NER was recently subjected to a severe test on the heavy mineral line between Shildon & Newport (Erimus yard). The train comprised of 17 vehicles weighing 460 tons maintained an average speed of 42 mph on a ruling gradient of 1 in 103 - equivalent to a drawbar pull of 6.5 tons. On a gradient of 1 in 200 it attained 58 mph - a drawbar pull of 5 tons and an overall average of 5.5 tons. Such results have not yet been produced on the same section of railway with a steam locomotive.

It was added to the stock list in May 1922.

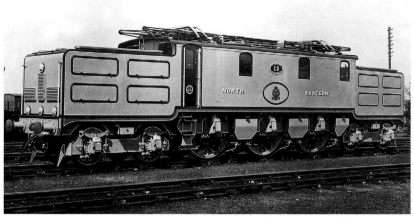
Electric 2-Co-2 passenger locomotive No. 13 in the paint shop yard at Darlington.
John Alsop Collection

What the above doesn't reveal is that No. 13 disgraced itself when on a demonstration run with 22 coaches behind it. R.A.S. Hennessy relates that the driver, Bill Hopper, had his doubts about the size of the contactors, thinking them to be too small. He backed his judgement by ordering a stand-by engine. The train headed off towards Bowesfield, followed by Sir Vincent in his personal coach. On the approach to Bowesfield the contactors burnt out and the procession ground to a halt. Sir Vincent arrived on the scene, was not best pleased and leaving no-one in doubt, headed back to Darlington and he gave the team responsible for No. 13 a week to have it operational.

Following the trials, No. 13 was 'mothballed' at Darlington. It was towed to Fighting Cocks to take part in the 1925 Centenary celebrations and thereafter made occasional demonstration runs for VIPs. It also put in an appearance at Open Days at various locations - Faverdale, Middlesbrough, Shildon and Darlington works over a period of four years. No. 13 was withdrawn from stock on 21st August, 1950 and went to Catcliffe near Rotherham on 15th December, 1950 where it was cut up.

Raven's enthusiasm for electric traction is reflected in the various papers that he produced and the lectures that he gave. The 25th January, 1921 saw him delivering a lecture to the York Railway and Debating Society on 'The Advantages of Electric Traction on Railways'.

We are informed that Mr R.L. (later Sir Ralph) Wedgwood was in the Chair and Raven's lecture was summarised as follows:

1. Increased acceleration
2. Higher scheduled speeds
3. More frequent service
4. Even tractive effort
5. Ease with which tractive effort can be adjusted to size of train
6. Higher mechanical efficiency and more constant efficiency during life
7. Small depreciation and maintenance cost
8. Increased capacity of existing tracks
9. Smaller amount of rolling stock required
10. Double heading with a single crew
11. Cleanliness

Detail of pantograph of locomotive No. 13.   *Doug Hardy*

The lecture was followed with rapt attention and a storm of warm and spontaneous applause rewarded the lecturer.

In the course of presenting a paper to the North East Coast Institution of Engineers and Shipbuilders in December 1921 he said:

> I have endeavoured to show in this paper the great advantage of being able to build or design a locomotive which by its tractive effort is able to keep a more uniform speed over the railway. In order to do this, it is necessary that you should be able to design a machine capable of giving you the power within the limits of the present load gauge. With a view to showing the difficulty of increasing the power of a steam locomotive without exceeding these limits as they stand to-day, I have worked out and show in diagram form an electric locomotive capable of exerting a pull of 15 tons which would haul a train of 1,000 tons up a gradient of 1 in 100 at 30 miles per hour, which is something I think we ought to aim at in the future; also a steam locomotive for dealing with the same work.
>
> It will be seen from the above that the one is within our present gauge and the steam unit considerably outside it and would be impossible to build unless a large amount of money were spent over widening the line and altering bridges and stations. It would require three of our two cylinder class 'T2' locomotives to do the work of this electric locomotive.

In June 1922 he addressed the Institute of Mechanical Engineers in Paris presenting a paper on 'Electric Locomotives' in the course of which he had to reassure his audience that 'they had not yet lost the author as a steam locomotive man'.

On 4th January, 1923 he spoke to the GWR (London branch) Lecture and Debating Society on the advantages of electric traction. The date is interesting as it was only three days after the Grouping and Raven was no longer a CME - only a Technical Adviser and he must have realised that he was tilting at windmills in his crusade for electrification. The ECML project had been abandoned and the newly formed LNER under William Whitelaw and H.N. Gresley was not particularly interested in any form of traction other than steam, but Gresley did suggest that one of the Shildon locomotives should be converted to diesel electric using a Beardmore engine. Raven soldiered on and in April 1924 delivered yet another homily on the advantages of electric traction, this time to Metropolitan Vickers Debating Society in Manchester. This seems to be a good example of preaching to the converted as Metro-Vick had supplied electrical equipment to the NER.

Eventually, Raven gave up the unequal struggle. It says something for his enthusiasm and tenacity that he persevered as long as he did - it also suggests that this single-mindedness of purpose blinded him to the realities of life as it was in 1919/20. He must have been aware when he returned from Woolwich of the dramatic changes that were in the pipeline. The Railways Act of 1921 was in its infancy but it was a lusty infant and it seems that Raven chose to ignore it and, in addition, to pay scant attention to the deteriorating economic situation. He must surely have been aware that not everyone was draped in the silks of wild and changing fashion; that hopes for a post-war boom were not realized because the Government's economic arithmetic was shot through with errors; that there were over one million unemployed and that their only weapon was strike action that led to the declaration of a state of emergency? In submitting his annual report for 1919, the Chief General Manager, R.L. Wedgwood, pointed out that in 1918 there was a 5 per cent reduction in total tonnage carried, there was very little war traffic, there had been various strikes and mineral traffic was down by 13.05 per cent. He notes that there was increasing competition from road traffic and that there was also an increase in the number of ships fuelled by oil.

He commented, 'The resources of the railway were heavily taxed throughout the year and the introduction of the eight hour day for railwaymen on 1 February 1919 added to our difficulties'.

In the light of Wedgwood's gloomy report it is surprising to say the least that further electrification was seriously considered. Declining revenue was not the prerogative of the NER - the Country was sliding inexorably towards depression and yet Raven was allowed, even encouraged, to press on with his plans when it should have been obvious that the economic climate was not in his favour.

He had had precious little support from his pre-Grouping fellow CMEs and one wonders how they viewed his obsession with electrification. Robinson of the Great Central Railway was not impressed with Raven's enthusiasm and yet here was a man who had been as adventurous as the next with his experiments in the realms of alternative fuels for steam locomotives. With the exception of the Liverpool and Southport (of the Lancashire & Yorkshire Railway) - which dead-heated with the Tyneside scheme - the GCR and Robinson showed little interest in electrification. It did not arrive on the former GCR system until 1931 with the electrification of the Manchester/Altrincham joint lines. At the time that Raven was developing the Shildon line, Gresley was at Doncaster with no thoughts of electricity clouding his mind. His instincts told him that steam was here to stay, at least for the foreseeable future so why become exercised over the whims and fancies of the NER? Thus, the GNR did not become involved in the passion - logically it had no need to. Much of its route mileage was through some of the best coal country in the UK. So, coal was there for the taking, it had to be mined at the right price, sold at the right price and transported, also at the right price and, in addition, several of the Directors had coal interests. So Gresley continued to build big engines that consumed vast quantities of coal and, it may be assumed, everyone was happy. His attitude towards electrification is summed up in F.A.S. Brown's seminal biography of Gresley. Electrification warrants two references - one about the Sheffield-Manchester electrification (which was implemented several years after Gresley's death) and the other about the replacement of coaching stock on the Newcastle suburban service. This is a pity as in 1923 Gresley inherited a successful - albeit small - system that could have been developed and used for experimental work: in addition he inherited plans for extending the network complete with No. 13 and coaching stock in store at York. Also he had Raven as a consultant had he chosen to use him. It can be argued that capital was in short supply and no doubt it was but there was enough of it about to build 40 Pacifics, the Garratt and the whitest white elephant of them all, the water-tubed 4-6-4 between 1924 and 1930. Had there been the will, surely finance could have been found to carry out further research on electrification? It may well be that there was a clash of personalities and that Gresley was in charge and he ensured that everyone knew it - he certainly did later in his career. But to be fair to Gresley, and the LNER, as Vesting Day for the Grouping approached, the NER appeared to lose interest in electrification. The advisory committee on electrification chaired by Sir Alexander Kennedy held its first meeting in July 1920 and was some 12 months late in reporting by which time the depression had arrived. Merz was a member of the committee and was vocal in his criticism of it. In fact he put the responsibility for the collapse of the York-Newcastle scheme squarely on the shoulders of the Kennedy committee. This is, however, somewhat simplistic. Even had the NER survived, the York-Newcastle scheme would probably have been abandoned. It would have been an unimaginable financial burden on a company serving the most depressed area in the Country. In 1930, seven years after the formation of the LNER, the introduction of the mercury rectifier meant that rotary converters that had to be manned became obsolete and were replaced by sub-stations - a significant step in the electrification of rail transport. In 1931 the Weir committee reported on the future of the Country's railways and echoed all that Raven had advocated 20 years earlier. Cold comfort for Raven.

Any municipality worth its salt had an electrically-operated tram system. There were three methods of supplying the power to the cars - overhead, between the tracks - the 'plough' system much favoured by the then equivalent to London Transport - and the surface-mounted Dolter system that occasionally killed horses. The point is that there was no lack of experience with electric traction and with the manufacture of ancillary equipment. And yet when the Great Eastern Railway was seriously considering electrifying its commuter lines, the CME, James Holden was instructed by his Directors to design and build a steam locomotive that could out-accelerate any existing electric locomotive over a given distance. He built the 'Decapod' an 0-10-0 well tank to prove his point (this is reviewed in detail in Chapter Eight).

Electrification on the Eastern section of the LNER, as the GER became, had to wait until Nationalisation. It is, in a sense, fortunate that Raven died the year before the Shildon line reverted to steam and the overhead and ancillary equipment was carted off to the scrap yard. One can only speculate as to his feelings had he seen his 'baby' demolished. On the other hand, three years later a start was made on the electrification of the Sheffield-Manchester line and one can imagine Sir Vincent looking down and with a smug expression - that can be forgiven - saying to Gresley 'I told you so'.

Conclusion

In *Electric Locomotives of the North Eastern Railway* the late Ken Hoole makes the point that the East Coast Main Line electrification came to fruition some 70 years after Raven had proposed it. Writing at the time that system was being commissioned he - Hoole - ends his conclusion thus, 'Electric locomotives are coming to the London-Edinburgh east coast route and let us hope that they will be a huge success - even if they are some 70 years late - but let us not forget Sir Vincent Raven and number 13'. And that says it all.

Chapter Seven

Labour Relations

Although the NER was well managed and successful, it was not immune from labour problems and indeed had a chequered history dating back to April 1866 when the Engine Drivers' and Firemen's United Society was formed. A strike was called, the NER drafted in blackleg labour and the union collapsed in April 1867.

The company had an ambivalent, if not downright puzzling, attitude towards the formation of trades unions. The above example illustrates one extreme and the introduction of the Darlington Programme, guaranteeing a 10 hour day, overtime at time and a quarter and separate rates for Sundays is another extreme and it is generally acknowledged that the NER was in the forefront of collective bargaining. When, in November 1889, a committee made up of some of the Directors failed to agree with a delegation of union officials and employees' representatives the meeting resulted in deadlock. Each side agreed on arbitration and Dr Spencer Watson was called in as arbitrator. There was an arrangement with the NER and the traders in Green Market, Gateshead that the company would service the market on what appears to be an *ad hoc* basis on Saturday mornings. The men were called out as required and the hours were irregular. Eventually the men objected and came out on strike on 21st February, 1897. Gibb and Butterworth met 25 delegates and the matter was resolved

The All Grades programme of October 1886 touched on a shorter working day and improved pay and at a meeting of General Managers and Chairmen at Euston the companies represented refused to negotiate, with the notable exception of the NER. Arbitration was called for and Lord James of Hereford was appointed arbitrator. The All Grades programme was similar in many ways to the Darlington Programme and Lord James's recommendations for shorter hours, improved overtime rates and separate agreements for Sundays were rejected out of hand by all of the participating companies - with the exception of the NER - with the terse comment 'not to yield in the slightest degree'.

The unpopularity of railways as employers reached its peak at the end of the 19th century and the Railway Companies (Prevention of Accidents) Act of 1900 didn't help. The Act was intended to protect employees whilst at work but the view was taken that the railways must be bad employers if the workforce needed the protection of the law to ensure safety.

In November 1907 Sir Walter Cunliffe, a Director of the NER, wrote to R.F. Dunnell, the company Secretary, tendering his apologies for absence at the November Board meeting. He continued, in a self-deprecating manner:

My opinion of railway matters in general are absolutely unworthy of a moment's consideration by the Directors, but I do feel, on general principles, I should be glad to see the North Eastern Railway Co come into line with the other great railways of the Country and not stand out alone in recognising the so-called Men's Union.

The postscript to the letter is equally revealing, 'I may add that the reason assigned here is that the stock has not risen in the same degree during the past few days since the settlement of the dispute with Mr Bell, is a fear that the NE will continue to dally with the union to the Company's ultimate disadvantage'.

The *North Eastern Railway Hours and Report* was produced in 1909. It consists of 258 pages and examines in minute detail the duties and wages of every grade of employee under Raven's aegis. Evidence was taken from drivers, firemen and inspectors and indeed from Raven himself. He asserts in his opening statement that wages and conditions for footplate men are better on the NER than on any of the Country's railways. (Bearing in mind that there were 119 of them that was something of a sweeping statement but it went unchallenged.) He then presented to the panel details of a day in the life of a driver, opening his remarks as follows: 'It is generally accepted that an Express Passenger Train driver's duties are the most arduous amongst driver's duties'. He then deftly attempts to prove otherwise and cites a typical shift for an NER driver who was booked to work the 3.06 am Newcastle-Edinburgh and the return working at 10.00 am, arriving in Newcastle at 12.36 pm. The driver signed on at Greenesfield shed at 1.46 am and signed off at 1.06 pm and for working an 11 hr 20 min. shift he received 10s. 5d. including bonus. Raven continues,

On analysing the work shown above, it will be seen that out of the 11 hrs 20 mins he was only working trains 5 hours 23 minutes or 47% of his time. The time running light was 50 minutes and allowing 95 minutes for duties at the beginning, middle and end of the shift, the man has really had 3 hours 31 minutes rest. This turn is representative of the express working between Newcastle and Edinburgh. The statement shows that the percentage of running time including light is 57.2%.

The next paragraph of Raven's statement is worthy of being reproduced in full:

Taking the hours actually working trains, even these hours are not laborious nor are they exacting. The man has an engine up to its work. The engines of to-day have a bigger boiler capacity enabling steam to be more easily maintained. The oldest and most experienced firemen are on these trains and the driver has no anxiety in that respect. Therefore, during the few hours that the driver is actually running trains, his work is made as light as possible for him. There is therefore in my opinion, no reason to suppose that the hours are too long for such work. Further, it would not be practical to work men on eight hour shifts on this service without booking the men off at Edinburgh, causing great expense to the Company and, at the same time, I should say, making the men suffer inconvenience that they are strangers to now. Even with the present hours it is difficult to fit the time in without booking the men off. It is the rarest thing for us to have an application from an express passenger man to come off express passenger work but, on the other hand, we have had cases where they have grumbled when we took them off through age etc. and gave them less important engines to work. This shows that they do not consider 10 hours a strain upon them.

Raven follows the above with an observation on the work of firemen. He notes that a fireman will move between four and five tons of coal during a shift on the Newcastle-Edinburgh express. He does not believe that this is 'beyond a reasonable day's work for which the pay with bonus is 6s. 9d.'

Raven then turns the spotlight on the goods and mineral working and states 'only about 50% of the turns reach even 50 miles per day. This, on a minimum shift, means that we are paying at the high rate of 7s. 6d. for a working equivalent of only 5 mph - *a tram driver does more*' [author's italics]. He ends this section by stating that the cost of awarding eight hour shifts to footplate men and motormen would add £160,000 to the wages bill and would require 73 extra engines.

On the subject of ballasting he writes,

> Ballasting is also paid for at the top rate. It is very easy work and 10 hours cannot be said to be too much for the men engaged on it and we consider that the work done ought to come under the 7s. limit for ten hours. The condition under which these men work of necessity causes them to stand about the major portion of their time and it is unreasonable to pay them as we are doing at main line rates [one cannot help wondering whether or not Raven had spent any time in a platelayers' hut at Stainmore Summit in the teeth of a north-easterly blizzard].

The assumptions made in the above reveal the dark side of Raven's attitude towards the men. There is a touch of arrogance about the comments which borders on the 'aren't they lucky to be working for the NER'. He follows this with a somewhat lame attempt to justify what has gone before: 'That an engineman's life is a healthy one is shown on Chart 1 to the supplement to the Registrar General's report, 1908, where they (enginemen) are fifth on the list with regard to longevity'.

The report comments on 'moonlighting' - not that that word is used - and Charlie Baister and J.H. Smeddle were instructed to prepare details of men who were engaged in 'private trading' and who were based at Gateshead and York respectively. The range of these illicit occupations is wide and varied from herbalist to Temperance Refreshment Room owner (in the wife's name of course); from publican to wet fish vendor. The report ends, rather ominously, that 'No permission was given for private trading'.

It was to be 10 years before the eight hour shift was introduced. Admittedly World War I delayed it although, for reasons stated, Raven and Wedgwood were in no hurry to implement the change.

Raven's half-yearly reports for December 1910, June 1911, and December 1911 mention strikes. In 1910 there was trouble with the carriage cleaners at Newcastle and he took £900 from his budget as a 'loyalty bonus' for non-strikers. In 1911 he reports that there was a strike of shunters at Thirsk, they were punished by 12 months' reduction in pay. He also notes, rather plaintively, that the Coronation of King George V and Queen Mary took £3,466 out of his budget.

In the summer of 1911 the Government was in trouble and was faced with its biggest strike. It was triggered by the seaman and the docks and railways soon followed suit. There were ugly scenes - the military used fixed bayonets against railwaymen and nine railwaymen were killed in Llanelli - six by an explosion in trucks that they were attempting to derail and three were shot. At its height 200,000 were on strike. It drifted to a close on 19th August but the NER did not settle until 23rd August. Raven notes that this took another £3,770 out of his budget.

In one of its leaders *The Times* noted, 'In short, the men won a striking victory. It is not complete but it goes a long way towards completion and very much further than anyone, not excepting the men themselves, ever expected'.

The year 1911 was a significant one. Lloyd George introduced his National Insurance Bill and, equally portentous, 1911 was the year when the employers began to recognise the unions. Had the NER acted quickly in this context, Raven would have been saved some awkward moments.

As brilliant an administrator and as outstanding an engineer as he was, Raven's weakness was in man management, especially in the area of the manual workers. This is hinted at in diary entries already quoted but his biggest gaffe came in 1912. He had been with the company 37 years, had worked his way through the departments and had been CME for two years and yet with all that experience, his inept handling of a situation precipitated a strike that became a *cause célèbre*.

On the afternoon of 26th October, 1912, Nichol Knox, a goods driver, booked off duty and went home for a meal. Later that evening he went for a drink and had two glasses of rum and hot water and he was subsequently arrested for being drunk and disorderly. Knox appeared before the Newcastle Bench on 5th November, 1912 and the Magistrates declared that they felt that the evidence was unsatisfactory on both sides. Nevertheless, he was fined 5s. for being drunk and costs were awarded against him.

Enter Raven. Early in December 1912 he sent for Knox and informed him that he was, as a result of being found guilty, to be down-graded to pilot driver with immediate effect with a reduction of 9s. per week in his pay and this some five weeks after the offence. This decision was supported by the General Manager, A. Kaye Butterworth, and as a result of the intransigence of his reply to the Gateshead men they were up in arms and voted by an overwhelming majority to strike in support of Knox from 7th December, 1912 despite the fact that their union secretary advised against it. The action which was described by the London *Evening Standard* as 'the right to get drunk' spread rapidly and by 9th December, 3,500 men were on strike. The strikers held that they had strong grounds for supporting Knox. They doubted that he was drunk on the night in question and they felt that there had been a miscarriage of justice because Knox was not due back on duty for 30 hours after the alleged offence. The strikers also averred that the company had no right to punish Knox for his behaviour when he was off duty. He had 37 years' service with the company, an unblemished record and, from his photograph, he appears to be the epitome of Victorian/ Edwardian rectitude.

In an article in the *Northern Echo* of 3rd December, 1912 headed 'Mr Raven's Position', Raven robustly defended his course of action. In the article he said that 'the question of the Company's right to enquire into a man's conduct apart from his working hours depended entirely on that man's duties'. He went on to say, 'In the case of a man employed in a duty which entails risk to the public, if he was not a sober and competent man, I take it that the Company must distinctly consider what his conduct is outside his hours of employment'.

Later in the article he states,

I have not dismissed the man. I have only put him on a pilot engine. This means that he is in the yard under the observation of officials of the Company who will be able to see whether he is capable of conducting himself properly. Because I do this the men say 'we are going out on strike'. If that is their humour then they are going out. I have no intention of giving way. If they must go on strike, they must go. There are times when one must take a firm stand.

Illustrated Chronicle

A DAILY PAPER WITH ALL THE NEWS AND PICTURES.

No. 828 (Registered as a Newspaper)   Saturday, December 7, 1912.   Price One Halfpenny.

STRIKE ON THE N.E.R.: MAN WHOSE CASE HAS CAUSED IT.

Left: This portrait of Nichol Knox was the cover photograph of the *Illustrated Chronicle* on 7th December, 1912.

Illustrated Chronicle

Below: Driver Nichol Knox attends to the lamp on the smokebox of 'E' class 0-6-0T No. 221.

Illustrated Chronicle

The response from the Gateshead men came at a meeting held on 10th December, 1912 and on 11th December, 1912, the *Newcastle Daily Chronicle* reported on it. The report is entitled 'Mr Raven's Removal'. It makes several points including the following:

> Mr William Fairless, who presided (at the meeting), said that he was not going to defend drunkenness, but he did contend that the company had no right to say what the men should do in their leisure time. If the men were going to allow a despot to dictate to the men in one department as to how their off-duty should be spent, the despotism would soon spread to other departments.

Later in the meeting Mr T. Kell moved the following drastic motion: 'That this meeting of railway workers calls upon their respective general secretaries to call their Executives together with a view to a general strike on the NER, and the removal of Mr Raven'. The motion was received with cheers. Mr Raven, said the speaker, had continually stood in the way of the workers. There was not a man in the shops who was not convinced that he was an obstacle and they must demand that Mr Raven be put in his proper place. It was because unionists and non-unionists alike believed this that the meeting had been thrown open and they asked for a unanimous vote. Mr Raven, declared the speaker, had done his uttermost to destroy the railway societies. Mr McDonald, Heaton Branch, seconded and said that there had been nothing but unrest upon the NER since Mr Raven was appointed to the position of chief mechanical engineer, simply for the reason that he was not a fair dealing man. The present trouble rested upon Mr Raven because if he had gone into the question properly, the deadlock would not have been brought about. A man who was not prepared to bring about a settlement when it could be done was no use to the railway workers, to the company or the shareholders and he should be removed (Cheers).

In supporting the motion, Mr R. Moffat, organiser for the GRWU said 'Were they going to allow one man to obstruct them or were they going to remove him out of their path? No community could afford to be obstructed by one man. Mr Raven could go up or down so long as he was got out of the way and the employees must make it their business to see that he was removed'. The resolution was carried unanimously and with cheers.

There had, of course, been much activity on the part of A. Kaye Butterworth, the General Manager and Walter Hudson, the MP for Newcastle. They travelled up and down to London and held interminable meetings and even involved the Lord Mayor of Newcastle in attempts to avert an all-out strike. The local papers reported every detail and printed a veritable plethora of readers' letters, the majority of which were very much in favour of Knox.

But this reporting had its lighter side. The juxtaposition of solemn warnings about the long-term effects of the strike and comments on the calibre of the magistrates with some of the advertisements were somewhat incongruous 'Dinneford's Magnesia - the best remedy for Acidity, Heartburn, Indigestion, Gout and Headache'. No doubt A. Kaye Butterworth *et al* drank it by the bottleful. Another incongruity is a bound volume with the following inscription in most impressive copperplate handwriting 'From W. Irving, Newcastle to Vincent L. Raven Esq. Chief Mechanical Engineer, N. E. Ry Darlington, 27

NORTH EASTERN RAILWAY.

RULES AND REGULATIONS

TO BE OBSERVED BY WOMEN IN THE

SHELL SHOP, DARLINGTON LOCO. WORKS

1. Time to be kept by the hour.

2. The week ends on Thursday at 5 p.m. and wages are paid at the end of the following week.

3. Working hours in this Factory 45 per week, as follows:

   No. 1 Shift starts on Sunday 2-30 p m. till 10-30 p m.
   Meal time 6-0 p.m to 6-30 p.m.

   No. 2 Shift starts on Sunday night 10-30 p.m. till 6-30 a.m.
   Meal time 2-0 a.m. to 2-30 a m.

   No. 3 Shift starts on Monday 6-30 a m. till 2-30 p.m.
   Meal time 10-0 a.m to 10-30 a.m.

   Those finishing on Saturday at 2-30 p m. start on Sunday at 2-30 p.m.
   Those finishing on Friday at 10-30 p.m. start on Sunday at 10-30 p.m.
   Those finishing on Saturday at 6-30 a.m start on Monday at 6-30 a.m.

4. An addition to the rate of pay at the rate of time and quarter will be paid to the shift commencing 2-30 p m. after 5-0 p.m., and to the shift commencing at 10-30 p.m. for the whole of the working hours. The same will apply to all Sunday duty with the exception that the addition to the rate of pay will be double time. Sunday duty ending at Midnight. Overtime will be paid for any hours worked in excess of the above named shifts at the usual rates applicable to the Locomotive Works provided 45 hours have been worked in that week.

5. Any woman not having obtained her check at the time appointed may come in not more than 15 minutes afterwards but will lose half an hour. Women are expected to be in their places ready for work when the bell is rung for commencing.

6. No woman will be allowed to begin or cease work at irregular hours except by special permission from the Foreman, and any woman losing more than one shift in one week will be liable on the second occasion to be suspended for the following shift or for the remainder of the week. Bad time-keeping will be held sufficient reason for dispensing with a woman's services.

7. Absence from work without leave or without satisfactory reason being given may be punished by dismissal.

8. On entering the works each woman will receive a metal check which she must leave at the place appointed every time she leaves the shop.

9. Any woman putting in a check other than her own will be liable to dismissal, and any woman failing to obtain her check before commencing work is liable not to be paid for the time so worked.

10. Any woman losing her check will be charged a penny for a new one.

11. Entering or leaving the works by any other way than the gate appointed is strictly prohibited.

12. Offences against the usual shop regulations or rules of propriety. damage, by neglect or carelessness, to Company's property, wasteful use of stores, &c., will be punished by fine, suspension, or immediate dismissal.

13. Except in cases of dismissal for misconduct, one week's notice on either side to be given previous to a woman leaving the service of the Company. Any woman leaving without such notice having been served will forfeit a week's wage.

14. "CAPS and uniforms are provided by the Company, and employees must wear them while at work."

BY ORDER,

VINCENT L. RAVEN,

CHIEF MECHANICAL ENGINEER.

Darlington, March 10th, 1916.

January 1913'. The contents, a complete set of press cuttings about the strike, just what Raven wanted.

An un-named Chemist calculated that Knox had drunk ⅖ of a fluid ounce of alcohol and an equally anonymous doctor wrote 'I cannot conceive it possible that any man in normal health would be affected by ⅖ ounce of alcohol unless he had previously been a total abstainer'.

On hearing of the case, General Bramwell Booth of the Salvation Army exhorted Knox to sign the pledge and, assuming that Knox complied, urged the company to re-instate him. The *North Mail* sent a reporter to Knox's Gateshead home 'with the object of ascertaining Mr Knox's opinion on the question'. It transpired that Knox was not at home 'but his wife was not long in expressing her opinion'. One has the impression that Mrs Knox was a feisty lady and sent the reporter off with a flea in his ear and a strong message for General Booth. Knox was seen later in the evening and confirmed that he had received a telegram asking him to sign the pledge. He further confirmed that he had no intention of signing the pledge, as he had no need to. 'Mr Knox quietly lit his cutty pipe and joined his mates further up the street'.

On 10th December, 1912, Alfred Thomas MP raised the case of Nichol Knox in the House and asked the then Home Secretary, Reginald McKenna,* to institute an enquiry. McKenna lost no time in setting it up and on the 13th December Chester Jones, the Home Office official appointed to conduct the enquiry, reported that the evidence that he had heard, 'totally failed to satisfy him that Knox was drunk and disorderly, that he was drunk and incapable or that he was drunk at all'. On the same day the King granted Knox a free pardon on McKenna's recommendation and the strikers returned to work when they were satisfied that Knox was to be fully reinstated. Apart from costing the strikers six days' pay, the 'Knox affair' underlined the inadequacy of the existing conciliation scheme and reminded management that the men could show militancy and solidarity as and when the occasion demanded. And yet the NER established a Conciliation Conference that held its first meeting on 30th March 1909 and by some sort of irony, Raven was appointed to the conference for three terms in January 1912, almost a year before the Knox affair. Thus, it would appear that Raven and his fellow members, Baister, Bengough, Geddes, Stamer and Wedgwood had not paid much heed to conference rules.

Also in 1909 the merger of the Great Central, Great Northern and North Eastern was mooted with a view to eliminating competition whilst retaining individual management. The proposals came to nothing although had they come to fruition, Geoffrey Hughes in his book *LNER* speculates on the prospect of Robinson Pacifics on the East Coast Main Line.

As is noted elsewhere, Raven was seconded to Woolwich Arsenal in 1915, returning to Darlington in 1919. It seems that problems with labour relations were to dog him throughout his career as he experienced strikes at Woolwich and, on his return to the North East, the men protested about eyesight tests that were carried out at Pilmoor and he had another strike on his hands.

---

* Reginald McKenna, the then Home Secretary and obviously a major player in the Knox affair achieved notoriety and had calumny heaped on him in 1913 with the introduction of the Temporary Discharge for Ill Health - the infamous 'Cat and Mouse' Act at the height of the Suffragette movement's activities. Many suffragettes were imprisoned, where they promptly went on hunger strike and were force fed. There was a public reaction to this so McKenna introduced legislation that enabled the authorities to release women from prison, but immediately their health improved they were re-arrested.

Chapter Eight

Chief Mechanical Engineer

The year 1910 was a memorable one. Dr Crippen added to his notoriety by being the first criminal to be arrested via radio, King Edward VII died as did Florence Nightingale. George V was crowned; Capt Scott and his team left for Antarctica on the same day that Raven reached the pinnacle of his career. Halley's Comet appeared - a good augury for Raven - not too special for Scott.

The *Railway Magazine* for December 1910 reported, somewhat belatedly, that Raven was appointed CME with effect from 1st June, 1910. The appointment was not calculated to provoke remark, as his career pattern up the company ladder had been as steady as it was predictable. The *Universal Directory of Railway Officials* of 1910 gives the following statistics and details of the senior management of the NER:

North Eastern Railway
Track miles - 1,722
Locomotives -2,000
Coaching stock - 4,648
Wagons - 111,717
Chairman - Rt Hon. J.A. Wharton
Deputy Chairman - Rt Hon. Lord Knaresborough
Chief Engineer - C.A. Harrison
Consulting Mechanical Engineer - Wilson Worsdell
Chief Mechanical Engineer - Vincent L. Raven
Assistant Mechanical Engineer - A.C. Stamer
General Manager - A. Kaye Butterwoth

Although the NER was one of the largest and wealthiest of the pre-Grouping companies, because it did not have a London terminus it was regarded by its competitors as a provincial railway. Be that as it may, when Raven took over, the area covered by the company ranged from Carlisle to Doncaster to Hull to Newcastle and with running powers to Edinburgh.

In these days of political correctness, it is somewhat difficult to accept that Raven succeeded Wilson Worsdell as a matter of course. It is obvious that he was groomed for stardom from an early age but even so there was no opposition, no advertising, no long listing and short listing, no interview. Instead all that appears in the minutes is as follows - minute 11707 dated 28th January, 1910:

Mr Wilson Worsdell having intimated his desire to retire from the position of Chief Mechanical Engineer at the end of May next
Resolved
That Mr Worsdell be appointed Consulting Mechanical Engineer to the Company from 1st June, 1910 until 31st December, 1911 at a salary of £2,000 per annum and that Mr Vincent L. Raven be appointed Chief Mechanical Engineer from 1 June at a salary of £2500 per annum.

And that was that.

The department that Raven inherited had its task well in hand and there were no immediate changes in design policy with reference to passenger and freight engines. In fact, between Raven's appointment and the formation of the LNER six major designs were introduced and, with the exception of the Pacifics, were built in numbers. Thus, Raven's department anticipated the needs of the motive power department rather than spend time and resources catching up.

A decision made early in Raven's tenure was to move the administrative offices to Darlington. Locomotive construction at Gateshead ended in 1909 and it was logical to concentrate new construction at Darlington. A parcel of land was acquired from the Stooperdale estate fronting on to Brinkburn Road and in due course the new offices were built and occupied in April 1912. That the building was, and still is, impressive is an understatement and the local paper waxed lyrical and likened it to a stately home. As the photograph shows, the offices were built in the Palladian style and had a curved drive 50 feet wide. It was as impressive inside as it was outside and consideration was given to the comfort of members of staff who worked there. 'Everything that careful expenditure, architectural skill and good taste could do was done in its construction and it remains a monument to the princely status of the North Eastern Railway' (O.S. Nock). The architect was Bell of York who was employed by the NER and who, during a career that spanned 57 years, designed buildings that ranged from the station hotels at York and Newcastle to what are regarded by some authorities to be amongst the finest rural stations in the country.

Writing from Palm Coast, Florida, a correspondent relates how he started work in the offices in 1932. He recalls that he was in the accounts department and was put in charge of a machine that printed out the names and numbers of all LNER employees in the North East. He continues, 'What a wonderful building Stooperdale was with those lovely revolving doors out front, wide stairways and hallways and spacious lifts. It was really great and it made you feel great working there'.

Nearer to home, another correspondent writes that there was a railway line that ran to the rear of the Stooperdale offices. She continues,

The line ended at a back entrance complete with concrete platform. This line was laid for the use of Sir Vincent Raven when travelling in the saloon coach that stood in readiness [for Raven] at platform three at Bank Top station and that Stooperdale was grandly appointed when it was built, to suit a man of his [Raven's] grand importance.

She adds that workmen came from Italy to lay the terrazzo floors and that during World War II air raid shelters were constructed under the flowerbeds and front lawns. She believes that some of them are still intact.

The official version for the use of the railway line at the rear of the Stooperdale offices is somewhat more prosaic: 'In the rear of the building is a railway siding from which fuel may be dropped from the tracks into the cellars of the new building'. The installation of this length of track was approved on 13th July 1911, minute 19128.

Apart from Raven's office, the building was home to A.C. Stamer's office, an army of clerks, the accounts department, a conference hall and on the first floor, Heads of Departments and, curiously, on the second floor adjacent to the

Jean Earle

Stooperdale offices, Brinkburn Road, Darlington looking very much as they did when they opened in 1910.

laboratories and materials testing department was the staff canteen. One wonders what happened to the offices on the first floor in the event of a chemical spillage or blocked drains and what system was in place to keep the fumes from the laboratories away from the kitchens and the canteen (especially the Directors' dining room!).

Of the Country's chief mechanical engineers some were outstanding, some were innovative and some have sunk without trace. Of the latter, one thinks of S.D. Holden who succeeded his father as locomotive superintendent of the Great Eastern Railway from 1st January, 1908, and did a prodigious amount of work on superheating. He resigned unexpectedly in a haze of whisky in 1912. Another example is Cecil Paget, appointed general superintendent of the Midland Railway in 1907 at a salary of £2,000 pa - his father, Sir Ernest Paget, happened to be Chairman of the MR - and went on to design and build the Paget locomotive. That this locomotive was innovative cannot be denied but its revolutionary sleeve valves seized whilst travelling at 60 mph. That and the intervention of World War I effectively ended Paget's career and sleeve valves were not tried again until O.V.S. Bulleid, that maverick CME of the Southern Railway, fitted them to his 'Leader' class locomotives in 1946. Paget and S.D. Holden were contemporaries of Raven's and he must have been aware of what they were or were not up to.

Raven had spent too much time with the NER to be as innovative as his contemporaries and his designs tended to follow established NER practice. There was no change in design policy largely because there was no need for change. The locomotives that he inherited were well up to the work required of them and such had been his influence on the locomotive department prior to becoming CME that traffic requirements were anticipated.

The Atlantics and a 4-4-4

Wilson Worsdell spent four years as a pupil at the Altoona works of the Pennsylvania Railroad. He paid a return visit in 1901 and came home impressed with the 4-4-2 locomotives that worked the principal expresses and as a result he introduced the 'V' class in 1903. The prototype was built at Gateshead, was designed specifically with East Coast traffic in mind and to replace the 'R' class locomotives which had to be double-headed on the main line expresses. It was followed by two more before the end of the year and by the middle of 1904 a further seven had been added to the fleet. Following trials with No. 532, the first of the class, they were allocated to express passenger work between Newcastle and York and Newcastle and Edinburgh.

The 'Vs' were big engines with a 5 ft 6 in. diameter boiler pitched 8 ft 1 in. above rail level. Additionally, the drive was onto the rear pair of coupled wheels and this necessitated 11 ft 4½ in. coupling rods, these dimensions giving the 'Vs' a massive appearance. As built, the cab roof on No. 532 was parallel with the boiler but was too low for the comfort of the crew and restricted forward vision. It was returned to Gateshead where modifications were carried out and these were reflected in the rest of the class.

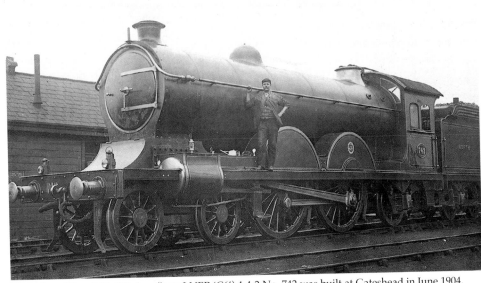

Wilson Worsdell's 'V' class (later LNER 'C6') 4-4-2 No. 742 was built at Gateshead in June 1904. This was one of only two engines of the class to survive beyond Nationalisation, being withdrawn in March 1948 having never acquired a British Railways number.

John Alsop Collection

Vincent Raven's 'Z' class (later LNER 'C7') 4-4-2 No. 2168. Built at Darlington in 1914 and withdrawn in May 1947.

John Alsop Collection

It is likely that Raven had a hand in some of the modifications. The 'V1s' were initially allocated to Gateshead but, as and when they were transferred to secondary duties, some went to Darlington and they were eventually withdrawn from Hull between 1944 and 1947.

With this background and the concomitant experience, Raven introduced his *magnum opus* - the 'Z' class Atlantics. As mentioned, they are regarded by the experts to be the best in appearance and performance of any of the North Eastern locomotives. At the time of their introduction, Darlington works was fully occupied building classes 'Y' and 'T1' with further orders in the pipeline. Thus, for the first time since McDonnell's reign, orders were placed with outside contractors, in this case the North British Locomotive Company who built 10 class 'Z' - saturated - and 10 class 'Z1' - superheated engines, in 1911. These were followed by 10 superheated engines in 1914 and a further 20 between 1915-1920. Thus, building continued during World War I at the time that Raven was away on Government service.

What was it about the Raven Atlantics that bestowed on them an excellent reputation that has stood the test of time? Ivatt of the GNR was of the opinion that if a locomotive looked right it was right and he was also of the opinion that the main measure of a locomotive's efficiency was its capacity to boil water. If these principles are applied to Raven's Atlantics then we have a clue to their success.

Whilst it is generally accepted that the 'Z' class Atlantics were the apotheosis of Raven's career, there is a curious comment at the end of an article by James Armstrong in the *North Eastern Express*, August 2001. Mr Armstrong states, 'Moreover, Raven's class 'Z' which came out in 1911 became notorious for their lack of hill climbing ability'.

This flies in the face of anything and everything written about the 'Z' class. Fortunately, this comment is more than countered by Dr W.A. Tuplin in *North Eastern Steam*. Never one to heap praise unnecessarily he writes,

> Bedecked in green and gold, a class 'Z' Atlantic was a magnificent embodiment of Edwardian ideas on the outward appearance of steam locomotives. [He continues] Form and colour combined to make a class 'Z' Atlantic a picture of taste and dignity. [and finally] This design was the climax of development of North Eastern steam. It was as much the last word in excellence as its designation was the last letter in the alphabet.

Raven was by now firmly wedded to three cylinders, to all cylinders driving onto the leading pair of coupled wheels and to Stephenson's link motion actuating piston valves. The cylinders and valve chests were in one casting and, of course, in common with all Raven's three-cylinder designs, there were three big ends and three eccentrics actuating three sets of valve gear on the leading axle, an arrangement that satisfied Raven but one that did not endear him to his design team nor to his maintenance staff. The three cylinders were 16½ in. in diameter and had a 26 in. stroke. The outside cylinders were tucked under the mainframes and were almost invisible. The locomotives were used on the mainline between York and Edinburgh, hauling the prestige trains and were not above the occasional return freight working. After the Grouping and following the introduction of Gresley's Pacifics, they were allocated to trains such as the Pullmans that were lighter than the core expresses.

Partially stripped cab of NER 'Z' class 4-4-2 No. 2163. Note the clutter surrounding the locomotive - what price health and safety!   *Northern Steam Photographs, Darlington*

During their working lives, and in common with many other classes, the 'Zs' and the 'Z1s' underwent various changes. The first 30 had conventional tenders with capacities of five tons of coal and 4,125 gallons of water; the next and final 20 had self-trimming tenders with coal capacity of 5½ tons. In addition, there were variations in the designs of the coal rails on the tenders and from the last member of the class, No. 2212, the coal rails sloped at the rear and this became standard for the NER and was continued after the Grouping by the LNER when building locomotives to NER designs. No. 2212 was built with Stumpf 'Uniflow' cylinders, in which the live steam and the exhaust steam followed the same route and did not alternate through ports as on locomotives with conventional valve gear - the steam moved in one direction only and was not exhausted at the same end of the cylinder as it entered. As with compound use of steam, the 'Uniflow' system was successfully used with stationary steam engines and it was tried, with little success, on a South Eastern Railway locomotive in the 1850s. It was revived by Professor Stumpf in Germany at the beginning of the 20th century. Various tests carried out with 'S2' class 4-6-0 No. 825 and 'Z' class No. 2212 did not justify further excursions into 'Uniflow' in terms of fuel economy and maintenance costs for two non-standard machines. No. 825 was rebuilt as a standard 'S2' and No. 2212 survived until 1935 when she was withdrawn, rebuilt with Lentz poppet valves and new cylinders and returned to traffic.

Raven followed the 'Zs' with the 'S2' class which was a development of Worsdell's 'S' and 'S1' classes, introduced in 1899/1901. The 'S' class was not a howling success despite the fact that one of the class, No. 2006, was sent to the Paris Exhibition of 1900 and was awarded a gold medal and a commemorative plaque although for what is not recorded. Opinions differ on the effectiveness of the 'S' class. In *Locomotives of the North Eastern Railway*, O.S. Nock comments that the trial run of No. 2001 was anything but inspiring and that members of the class were, in reality, no better than the Wilson Worsdell 'R' class 4-4-0 locomotives and in *North Eastern Steam*, the good Dr Tuplin actually agrees with O.S. Nock insofar as Tuplin avers that 23.7 square feet of grate area hampered by a shallow ashpan and no rear air inlet meant that the 'S' class could not run as fast as the 'Rs'. Worsdell was aware of the shortcomings of the class and in 1900 introduced the 'S1s'. The modifications included 8¾ in. piston valves and 6 ft 1 in. driving wheels. But even the 'tweakings' did not put the 'S1s' ahead of the 'R' class on express passenger workings. After the initial batch of five, no more were built.

Armed with 10 years' experience of the 'S' and 'S1' classes, Raven introduced the 'S2'. This was another 'tweaking' exercise and the 'S2' class differed from the 'S' class in that the boiler was 9 in. larger in diameter, superheaters were fitted as were piston valves. The class was designed as a true mixed traffic class and a favourite turn for the 'S2s' was the 12.30 pm Newcastle-Liverpool as far as York, the return working being the 3.50 pm Scotch Goods. The first seven members of the class were saturated but from No. 979 Raven fitted superheated boilers, he also conducted extensive trials with Nos. 786, 788 and 797 in 1913/1914. His main concern was evaluating superheating, comparing standard injectors, exhaust injectors and the Weir feed pump fitted to No. 788.

Raven Atlantic No. 2212 built at Darlington in 1918. This locomotive was rebuilt by Gresley in 1936 with Lentz poppet valves and reclassified as 'C7/2', withdrawal came in October 1945.

John Alsop Collection

Wilson Worsdell 'R' class 4-4-0 No. 2026 on an express passenger working.

John Alsop Collection

Wilson Worsdell 'S' class 4-6-0 No. 2003 (classified by the LNER as 'B13') was one of the original batch of the class, being built at Gateshead from 1899. This engine was withdrawn in July 1931.
John Alsop Collection

Raven 'S2' class 4-6-0 No. 786 at Beningborough on a Scottish express. This was the first member of the class to be built, at Darlington in December 1911, withdrawal came in December 1946.
John Alsop Collection

The final member of the 'S2' class was No. 825 which was built at Darlington in March 1913 and was fitted with the distinctive Stumpf 'Uniflow' cylinders. The 'Uniflow' cylinders were removed in March 1924 and the locomotive gave another 20 years' service in more conventional form. This picture was taken in Darlington paint shop yard.

John Alsop Collection

The final member of the class, No. 825, was fitted with Stumpf 'Uniflow' cylinders and it was subjected to extensive tests. It was, incidentally, fitted with Walschaerts valve gear, the only locomotive thus equipped in the history of the NER. Re-classified 'B15' on the formation of the LNER, 70 'S2s' were built between 1910-1924 and underwent various modifications at the hands of both Gresley and Thompson. With one exception, the class survived to enter British Railways ownership, the exception being one of the class that was destroyed in an air raid.

But there were things other than the development of steam and the promotion of electrification. A memorandum dated 17th November, 1910 and addressed to the General Manager dealt at some length with the comparative costs of repairing/replacing the company's wagons and those of private owners. During his career, Raven had shown some interest in the development of rolling stock but in the main choosing to leave it to the drawing office and the ever faithful Stamer. He must have been aware, however, that on succeeding Worsdell the buck had nowhere else to go and the request from Gibb, supported by Lord Airedale, had to be complied with. The report shows Raven to be cost-conscious as ever and he used the years 1898 and 1905 with which to compare building/repairing costs using Pease and Partners as a paradigm of private owners. In 1898, outside contractors quoted £91 15s. per unit for 12 ton goods wagons whereas Raven quoted £85 per unit built in the company's works at Shildon. Moving to 1905, he notes that the lowest tender received for 12 ton goods wagons was £113 per wagon, the company's price being £102 10s. 0d. if built at York. He was quick to point out in each case the specification was identical and that if the wagons were to be built at Shildon, the cost would be £93 5s. the difference in cost accounted for by the fact that Shildon made its own ironwork. He further pointed out that on a total of 500 wagons built in the company's workshops as opposed to outside contractors there was a saving of £12,000. He notes that 'the wagons were not ordered on account of their excessive cost'.

Raven then turned his attention to repairs. This section of the report opens with the following paragraph:

> A Railway Company's cost of repairs covers damage to its own wagons and to private owner's wagons in addition to wear and tear of its own stock. A Private Owner whose wagons are running on Railway Companies lines has nothing but wear and tear to pay for. If a Private Owner's wagon is damaged the Railway Company bears the cost, not the Private Owner.

He then analyses the cost of wagon repairs for the years 1900-1910 and quotes £2 17s. 1d. per wagon per annum for the company's wagons and £3 16s. 10d. for repairs to Messrs Pease and Partners wagons. The report ends rather abruptly.

At the same time that Raven was sorting out the above, he was occupied in producing a tank engine intended to work over Stainmore to Tebay and he introduced a good-looking three-cylinder tank engine with the unusual 4-4-4 wheel arrangement. The introduction of, and the problems with, the 4-4-4s throws into relief the lack of co-operation between the CMEs of the various companies. Each ploughed his own furrow and whilst each was no doubt aware of what the others were up to, it would, on occasions, have been advisable to

Raven's final 4-6-0 design was the 'S3' class, the first members of the class were built shortly after World War I. No. 927 stands at the coaling stage at York. The class was originally intended for use on fast goods services, with driving wheels of just 5 ft 8 in. in diameter. This locomotive was built in 1920 and survived until 1961 as BR No. 61422. *John Alsop Collection*

'S3' class (by this time classified LNER 'B16') No. 915 on the overhead crane, about to pass over an ex-Hull & Barnsley 0-6-2T (LNER class 'N13') at North Road works Darlington.
Northern Steam Photographs, Darlington

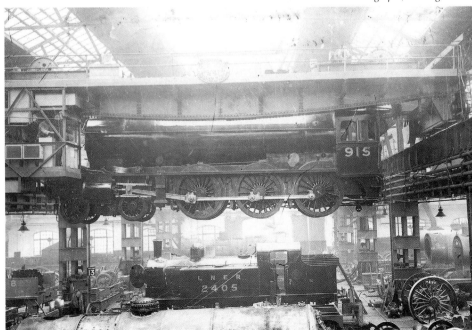

An unrebuilt Raven 'S3' in LNER days being coaled up at an unknown location.

Author's Collection

Class 'D' 4-4-4T No. 2143.

John Alsop Collection

LNER class 'A8' 4-6-2T No. 69860 was rebuilt by Nigel Gresley from Raven 'D' class 4-4-4T No. 2153 in August 1934, and as a 4-6-2T continued in traffic until June 1960.

Clive Field Photo Archive

contact a fellow CME and draw on his experience. Admittedly, Raven and Ivatt were 'lent' to the NBR but that was with the approval of their respective Boards. In 1896 E.G. Barker, CME of the Wirral Railway, introduced the 4-4-4 tank engine. The design was not successful and was not perpetuated and yet 17 years later Raven decided that the NER needed a 4-4-4T - the class 'D'.

The external appearance on the driver's side was somewhat spoiled by the presence of the Westinghouse pump and the steam reverser. The class as a whole was light on its feet and this caused some problems on greasy rails. In addition, the engines were reputed to roll at speed but despite these alleged shortcomings, 44 were built in eight years, including the years of World War I. Various modifications were made to members of the class culminating in all of them being rebuilt as 4-6-2 tank engines by Gresley following the successful conversion of No. 2162 (LNER number) during 1930/1931. Following evaluation trials, it was decided, reluctantly, that the 4-4-4s were not suited to the steeply graded Stainmore summit, but they did sterling work on passenger duties between Darlington and Saltburn, Saltburn and York and so on. And touching on Saltburn, a bizarre modification was the experimental fitting of a silencer to the Westinghouse pump of No. 2161 (LNER) to placate and mollify the good people of Saltburn who complained of the noise of the pump.

Away from locomotives and wagons a very interesting minute 994, appears in the proceedings of the Locomotive and Stores Committee, 16th May, 1912:

> The General Manager explained the circumstances which in his opinion rendered it desirable that the Company should purchase a house at Darlington for the Chief Mechanical Engineer and stated that a suitable house viz 'Grantly' in Carmel Road was now in the market and could probably be purchased at *from £4,000-£4,500* [author's italics].
> Resolved
> That the committee recommend to the Board that the Company should authorise the Estates Agent (A.G. Stevenson) to negotiate for the purchase of the house in question on the understanding that he (Raven) pays a suitable rent for the house and that his salary is increased *to £3,000 a year* [again, author's italics].

The Board approved.

'Grantly' was duly purchased and the Ravens moved from Alpine Cottage in Whessoe Street. This in itself underlines not only the high esteem in which Raven was held but also how wealthy was the NER at the time. At current prices (2004) informed opinion puts the property value of 'Grantly' at approximately £1,000,000. The Ravens lived at 'Grantly' from 1912 until they retired to Hampshire in 1923. Built in 1899, as the photograph shows, the design of the house does not appear to have been influenced by any particular school of architecture. Its first occupant was George Newby Watson, solicitor and Clerk to the Local Justices and who was the father of George Watson. The latter followed his father as Clerk to the Justices and also became Raven's son-in-law.

The house underwent various changes of use - and also of name as at sometime over the years 'Grantly' became 'Grantley' - that included a residential staff college for railway employees opened by the LNER in 1944 and continued as such until 1986 and it ended its days as a nursing home. Plans

'Grantly', Vincent Raven's residence.

'Grantly' in 2002.

Jean Earle

were submitted for re-development of the site and a demolition order dated 19th February, 2001 was carried out. The 1¾ acres formerly occupied by 'Grantly' have been re-developed with four houses occupying the site.

Operating in tandem with 'Grantl(e)y' as a residential training centre was Faverdale Hall which was bought by the NER in 1913 for £25,000 and became the home of A.C. Stamer. It was on the market in October 2001 for £500,000.

With an income of £3,000 pa, life must have been very comfortable. The Ravens involved themselves in the social life of Darlington and 'Grantly' was the setting for soirées and which were attended by what Sir John Betjeman would describe as 'the carriage folk'. Raven increased his involvement with the community and the municipality when he stood as a candidate for election to Darlington Borough Council. In his address to the electorate of the ward he noted that there were tramways, electricity, gas and water undertakings and the town's sewage disposal system in which the Corporation had invested heavily and that his engineering experience would be of value in the management of these utilities. There is no reference to any political party and following the poll he was elected with a majority of 458 over his only rival.

This victory was however short-lived. In spite of the exigencies of the war, Darlington local authority was going through the process of extending its boundaries and becoming a County Borough. To mark this, Councillor Pease was elevated to the Aldermanic bench and this necessitated a by-election in the West Ward to fill the vacancy only three weeks before the election of a full council of 24 members representing the voters of eight wards. If the letters pages of the *Northern Echo* in March 1915 are to be believed, there was little short of rioting in the streets at what was perceived to be a waste of ratepayers' money. But despite this plethora of protestations, the election had to go ahead at an estimated cost of £1,200. Thus Raven found himself defending a comfortable majority but this time there were four candidates for three seats. In addressing the voters, he remarked dryly that he had not changed much in a fortnight and that he had not had much time to misbehave. As the voters had had confidence in him then he hoped that the situation hadn't changed. The results of the poll showed that the confidence was still there as he came second with 972 votes only four behind Major B.D.G. Briggs.

There was obviously a question hanging over Raven's eligibility to serve on the council in view of his secondment to Woolwich and the Town Clerk of Darlington sought guidance from the Government Board. The substance of the reply was that Raven's position should be considered as his being on active service. Raven wrote to the Mayor stating that 'if it was the absolute desire of the Council that he should remain one of its members he would have much pleasure in agreeing'. He attended his first council meeting for four years on 3rd January, 1919 and was welcomed by the Mayor, Alderman Bates. The *North Star* reported the event and noted that in replying to the Mayor, Raven said he hoped it would not be long before they had a peace satisfactory to the nation and the rest of the world and that the sacrifices that had been made (and Raven had lost his younger son) would have a beneficial effect on the country. Between July 1917 and the end of 1922 he was an Acting JP for the County Borough of Darlington.

Two views of Faverdale Hall, Darlington in 1963.

Right: Raven's reminder to the electorate of Darlington West ward.   *Gordon Coates*

DARLINGTON MUNICIPAL ELECTION.

WEST WARD.

MR. VINCENT L. RAVEN

Respectfully Solicits your Vote and Interest.

He became a Freemason when he was initiated into the Percy Lodge, Newcastle-upon-Tyne and on moving to Darlington he became a joining member of The Marquess of Ripon Lodge on 1st November, 1894 sponsored by Dr George Middlemiss, a local GP and Thomas - later Sir Thomas - Putnam the managing director of Darlington Forge. The Marquess, after whom the lodge was named, was a prominent Freemason, Grand Master 1870-1874 and was very keen on improving the lot of the 'deprived classes' particularly in the realms of education. Raven too, was interested in education and this interest, especially in technical education led him, almost naturally, to Darlington Technical College. Minute 11666 dated 28th May, 1909 approves of his appointment to the Governing Body of which he eventually became Vice-Chairman. He was involved with the development of a steam/mechanical laboratory and in April 1913 was invited to open it. His keynote speech on that occasion was over-long and tedious. As might be expected there was a degree of Edwardian/Victorian moralizing, the value of the work ethic and exhortation to self-motivation contained in the speech. This is not surprising as Raven was a product of the Victorian age. His values and attitudes were shaped by his background, by his work experience and by what was happening in the world around him. As he reached maturity, he entered what is considered by social historians to have been the Golden Age of Gracious Living always assuming that there was the wherewithal to live graciously. Fortunately, in Raven's case there was.

In addition to the above community-oriented commitments, he was appointed to the Company's superannuation committee, Darlington section, on which he served until 1915.

Two appointments that are worthy of note were made at this time if only to put salaries into perspective. In February 1911 Captain W.F. Horwood was appointed Chief of Police for the entire NER system at a salary of £500 pa, Geddes was appointed deputy General Manager from 1st September, 1911 at a salary of £3,000 pa (this was in addition to his post as Chief Goods Manager). R.L. Wedgwood was appointed to the latter post in January 1912 with a salary of £1,500.

Carriage and Wagon Work

In 1899 the idea of separating King's Cross and Newcastle passenger traffic from the Scottish traffic was suggested and between then and 1912 there was a series of meetings that approved not only the design of the stock for the GN/NE joint operation but also details such as which of the two companies should pay for cleaning. The details and dimensions of the coaches built between 1905 and 1912 are well enough documented elsewhere and both Gresley and Raven attended the meetings in the company of, amongst others, A. Kaye Butterworth, and Oliver Bury and broad agreement was reached on designs, details and operating strategies. In total, 36 vehicles were built between 1905 and 1912 and even attempting to read between the lines there does not seem to have been discord until 31st January, 1912 when Raven had a meeting in Darlington with Gresley at which there seems to have been a degree of in-fighting as Gresley would not agree to NER brake gear and Raven was not happy with GNR underframes. (It doesn't take too much imagination to visualize the two engineers sitting opposite each other and blowing through their respective moustaches.) There was, eventually, agreement on drawing 1483 and one compromise was that the NER and the GNR would use their own WCs!

The NER - and Raven - was not particularly adventurous with passenger stock. Smoking was as contentious an issue in the mid-19th century as it is early in the 21st century and before the introduction of The Regulation of Railways Act 1868 decreed that accommodation for smokers must be provided on trains with one coach of each class, some companies instructed their servants to remove passengers caught smoking. Also in 1868 the Great Northern built the first coaches for the East Coast Joint Stock trains, the participating companies being the Great Northern, the North Eastern and the North British. These were six-wheeled vehicles and although the North British introduced sleeping cars on bogies in 1873 (built by the Great Northern) bogie coaches were slow to catch on and the NER was by no means in the vanguard. In 1900 it was decided that new stock was required for the 'Flying Scotsman'. Two trains were built with 65 ft-long coaches carried on six-wheeled bogies with the NER building the coaches at York and the GN building the restaurant cars at Doncaster. Twelve-wheeled stock followed Gibb's visit to the USA in 1902. C.J. Allen comments that the American influence was plain to see and that the coaches were 'comfortable but ugly'.

The NER built less corridor stock than any other British railway - apart from the London, Brighton and South Coast - but it did produce a batch of 52 ft-long coaches with clerestory roofs for suburban traffic. They were handsome corridor/non-corridor vehicles with internal corridors that gave access to the WCs but did not have vestibule connections. On 4th August, 1910 - shortly after Raven's appointment as CME - he was instructed by the Locomotive & Stores Committee to 'consider the effect of limiting the output of new carriages by an equivalent of 80 bogie carriages instead of 100 (as shown on the programme) and to report to the committee at its next meeting'. At the same meeting it was recommended that 3,163 goods and mineral wagons be built in the company's shops during the half-year ending 31st December, 1910. A memo also dated 4th August, 1910 from A. Kaye Butterworth refers to an estimate dated 7th May, 1908 entitled 'Future trends in Passenger Traffic and Carriage Building' and the gist of which projected an increase in passenger traffic that would require 130 new carriages per year for seven years. The estimate was considered to be on the high side and 'if adhered to may result in carriage stock increasing in a greater ratio than passenger traffic. Proposed to modify the previous recommendation and to limit the building programme to 100'.* Raven replied 'If he (Raven) were to receive an order of this kind he will, by transferring a number of his men from carriage building to wagon building, be able to keep the remaining men in the carriage shops fully at work throughout the year'. This altruistic gesture ensured that there would not be any redundancies and that when things returned to normal, the workforce would be in place.

---

* A. Kaye Butterworth's memo appears to conflict with that of the Locomotive & Stores Committee. No doubt he knew that the Locomotive & Stores Committee had made its request and he wanted to have his two penn'orth.

On balance, however, the NER was more interested in goods and mineral stock - hardly surprising when the geographical area covered by the company is considered. To the north-west was Consett with its heavy industry, to the south was Teesside with its equally heavy industry and in between was the Durham coalfield. Additionally, the absorption of the Hull & Barnsley Railway in 1922 brought with it access to the South Yorkshire coalfield. The Hull & Barnsley Railway (H&BR) had been a thorn in the flesh of the NER who strongly opposed its construction from its inception in 1879. The intention was to follow the route of two previously proposed railways - the Hull & Barnsley Junction and the Hull & West Riding Junction - and to terminate at a deepwater dock constructed in Hull with the express purpose of shipping coal. It had a chequered history, finding itself in receivership in 1887 but recovering sufficiently to be able to pay a dividend in 1913 and to fulfil a useful purpose in transporting coal from the Barnsley area to Hull docks. C.J. Allen makes the point that even taking into account declining coal traffic, the former H&BR was one of the first lines to be closed by British Railways and without any detriment to Hull.

At the beginning of World War I the wagon stock stood at 118,000 of which 59,815 were mineral wagons and this reflects the type of traffic. Raven tried his hand at designing wagons with a 20 ton coal/coke wagon. This was followed by a 40 ton version which in turn was followed by a variety of bogie wagons for the transporting of steel in its various guises - bolster bogies for rails and plate and well wagons for castings and special wagons for out-of-gauge loads.

Raven went on to design all-steel kitchen cars for the ECJS including the North British Railway. Three were built at York and the all-steel construction was influenced by the inadequacy of the existing electricity supply. In a memorandum Raven wrote,

> Owing to the difficulty of procuring sufficient current for an efficient electrical cooking installation, gas is used and it was decided with a view to reducing the liability of conflagration to a minimum to build these vehicles of steel.

Paternalism at the workplace is not a popular concept at the beginning of the 21st century and yet 100 years ago it was, certainly with large companies, normal practice. There were of course, covert conditions and strictures. Throughout the company there was a well-defined pecking order and this would be a reflection of class-ridden society outside the workplace.

The NER was no exception and in general, its workforce was well looked after provided the employees knew their respective places and adhered to them - the management was quick to show its disapproval of any departure from what was regarded as the norm - (*vide* Raven's diaries). On the other hand, the NER was on occasions forward-looking in its treatment of its employees. For example, in 1875 the Board voted six months' wages to the widow of an employee who had died whilst in the company's service, it voted a donation of £5 to the widow of 'John Peal, engine driver, who died from illness brought on by exposure to the recent frost' and recommended that 'half wages be allowed for six months to W. Mews, gatekeeper at Haydon Bridge who is incapacitated by age'. There are also several examples of the Board showing consideration to its employees, especially platelayers who, it would seem had a life expectancy similar to that of a Battle of Britain pilot. Yet when, in 1893, the secretary of Gateshead branch of the Amalgamated Society of Railway Servants applied to the Traffic committee for the provision of overcoats and Wilson Wordsell applied at the same time for protective clothing for 'wagon greasers, oilers, inspectors and other outside workers', the minute book states: 'Application declined (18055)'. There are inconsistencies, however. An entry in Raven's diary dated 5th November, 1904 reads as follows:

> Delegation of wagon greasers and examiners - Shildon. President Mr Thackery: Geo Hick and W. Bibby representing the men. Offered which men accepted to give 11 hours for a day's work with meal hour. Mens' wages to rise to 24s. and 18s. per week. Agreed to pay them for a day for coming to see me.

Now this entry, when compared with those already quoted is interesting insofar as it sheds a new light on Raven's character. His attitude towards the men appears to have mellowed somewhat and yet subsequent events contradict this and the 'hard man' comes to the fore. Another anomaly is minute 11694. It states that 'officers and clerical grades who reach the age of 67 years on or before 31st December, 1909 will be allowed to continue for one more year'. This was repeated in 1910, 1911 and 1912, an interesting forerunner of doing away with ageism before the word was coined.

There were, however, anomalies that would not be tolerated today and are prominent in differentials in the salary/wage structure. The wages book for Raven's office from 1909-1914 reveals striking differentials and very little increase in wages during that period. For instance, the chief clerk in charge of the general office received £250 pa., the clerk in charge of the mileage office at Gateshead received £300 pa, whereas his chief female clerk was paid a paltry £75 pa. Locomotive inspectors first class (ex-drivers) received £156 pa, second-class £130 pa.

The 'T' class 0-8-0 freight engines

At the end of the 19th and the beginning of the 20th centuries, goods and mineral traffic on the NER was increasing and there was a need for heavy freight engines.

Worsdell realised that eight-coupled locomotives would be the answer, but what form should they take - 2-8-0, 0-8-0, inside or outside cylinders? The outcome of his deliberations was the 'T1' class, an outside-cylindered 0-8-0 equipped with piston valves. He reasoned that it was important to have as much adhesion weight available as possible on the coupled-wheels and that the leading overhang at the front end would not be a disadvantage as the engines would not be travelling at speed. Ten engines came out of Gateshead in 1901, followed by another 10, but this batch was fitted with slide valves. Then came a further 30 with piston valves and finally, as a result of dynamometer car tests carried out in 1906 with a 'T' and a 'T1' it was realised that piston valves were not necessary on slow moving freight engines. In 1907 from Darlington works

Wilson Worsdell's 'T' class 0-8-0 (later LNER class 'Q5') No. 2118 with 4 ft 7¼ in. driving wheels. This engine was one of the first batch, built at Gateshead in 1901.   *John Alsop Collection*

Vincent Raven's 'T2' class 0-8-0 (later LNER class 'Q6') No. 1247 also with 4 ft 7¼ in. driving wheels. This engine was the first member of the class to built, in February 1913, and it continued in service until July 1963.   *NELPG Collection*

came a further 40 with slide valves. It is generally accepted that the power behind Worsdell's throne was Walter Mckersie Smith, the chief draughtsman and a great advocate of piston valves, a type of which he invented. This could well account for the chopping and changing of valve gear. The locomotives equipped with piston valves were classified 'T' and those fitted with slide valves were 'T1' and this was the position when Raven took over.

Following a conference on superheating in 1913, some 14 years after Aspinall of the Lancashire & Yorkshire (L&Y) fitted a smokebox-type superheater on his 4-4-2 No. 737 and some seven years after Hughes, also of the L&Y, fitted Schimdt superheaters to a series of 0-6-0s, Raven became convinced that superheating was as effective on freight engines engaged on long hauls as it was on passenger engines. As a result, when the need arose for another batch of 0-8-0s, some two years after his appointment, the 'T2s' emerged from Darlington works, the first being No. 1247 in February 1913. They were variations on the 'T1s' insofar as the boilers were slightly larger, they were superheated, had 8¾ in. piston valves and steam brakes. O.S. Nock describes the 'T' class as 'grand engines'. Ken Hoole writes that 'The T2 engines proved to be one of Raven's best designs' and W.A. Tuplin chips in with 'That class T2 was "successful" [sic] may be judged from the fact that 120 engines were built in eight years with only trifling departures from the original design.'

The above-named writers agree on other aspects of the 'T2s' - that they thrived on neglect and that they made a tremendous contribution to victory in both World Wars. Furthermore, 17 of them lasted almost to the end of steam, being withdrawn in 1967. The 'T3s' were not so fortunate, all 15 were withdrawn in November/December 1962.

The 'Ts' were designed with the nature of the road over which they would be operating very much to the fore. It is recorded that in 1902 a train of 1,326 tons hauled by an unidentified 'T1' was worked from Stella Gill to Tyne Dock, a distance of 11 miles, at an average speed of 21 mph. Stella Gill was the point at which coal from the neighbouring collieries was concentrated and then transported to Tyne Dock and loaded onto ships. The gradient varied from 1 in 250 to a rapid descent of 1 in 47 at the Dock. In the reverse direction, another unidentified 'T1' worked a train of 60 empties out of Tyne Dock and the train was then augmented by an extra 20 wagons for the run to Stella Gill.

The 'Ts' worked over most of the northern lines of the NER including West Auckland to Stainmore and Kirkby Stephen to Tebay with gradients varying from level at West Auckland to 1 in 59 at Stainmore Summit.

Fifty of the locomotives equipped with slide valves were requisitioned by the Railway Operating Department during World War I and shipped to France in 1917. They were considered to be amongst the best - if not the best - of the 0-8-0s sent to France and their commodious cabs and steam reversing gear were much appreciated. On their return, they were overhauled, put back to normal duties and in addition to being repainted, they were embellished with a replica of a bursting grenade and three stripes.

Raven 'T2' class (as LNER 'Q6') 0-8-0 No. 2238 on a lengthy train of mineral wagons near Blaydon.   *NELPG Collection*

Raven 'T3' class (later LNER 'Q7') 0-8-0 No. 901, this engine was the first of the class built at Darlington in 1919. It remained in service, along with all but two of its classmates, until December 1962.   *John Alsop Collection*

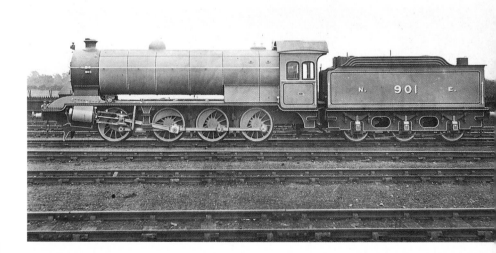

Raven 'Q6' class 0-8-0 No. 63395 at Sunderland South Dock in September 1967. This locomotive was later preserved (*see Chapter Eleven*).   *Clive Field Archive*

Raven 'Q7' class 0-8-0 No. 63468 near Three Horse Shoes signal box, West Boldon on a Tyne Dock-Consett train.   *John Clewley*

'W' class 4-6-0T No. 695.   *John Alsop Collection*

'W1' class 4-6-2T No. 693 is seen at Scarborough shed. This locomotive had been rebuilt into this form with extended frames and a longer bunker in February 1916. By January 1917 all 10 members of the class had been rebuilt.   *John Alsop Collection*

The 'W' class 4-6-0T engines (subsequently re-built as 'W1' class 4-6-2T engines)

As the class 'O' 0-4-4T engines were having difficulty in coping with the steeply-graded route between Middlesbrough and Scarborough, Worsdell introduced the 'Ws' in 1907. He had considered a 2-6-2 design as used by Churchward on the GWR but there was no tradition for outside cylinders on the NER. In any case, platform clearances on the Scarborough line might well have been too restrictive to allow a tank engine with outside cylinders and coupled wheels of the correct diameter to supply the power needed to operate trains over the line.

An alternative was a 2-6-2T with inside cylinders. The Lancashire & Yorkshire Railway was the only company to utilize this particular type of locomotive and the experience gained was not encouraging. Thus, Worsdell found himself, not for the first time, in a dilemma. He resolved it in a curious way by introducing the 'W' class of 4-6-0 tank engines. Ten were delivered in 1907/08 and put to work in the Leeds-Wetherby area, the reason being that the civil engineer had not completed the strengthening of some of the bridges on the coastal route. In *North Eastern Steam* Dr W.A. Tuplin is of the opinion that the 'Ws' as built did not look right and were not right. He notes that the bunkers were too small, holding only 2½ tons of coal - insufficient for a day's work. The problem was solved by Raven. He enlarged the bunkers to hold four tons and provided pony trucks. The modifications were carried out between 1915 and 1917 during the time that Raven was on war service.

The 'W1s' were eventually displaced by 'A8' class 4-6-2Ts and then worked all over the North Eastern area of the LNER.

The 'X' class 4-8-0T shunting engines

Although three-cylinder propulsion had been toyed with during the 19th century - it was introduced by Robert Stephenson in 1846 for the Berwick & Newcastle Railway - Holden's 0-10-0 well tank, the short-lived 'Decapod' was the first successful three-cylinder simple locomotive. It was built to prove that steam traction could at least equal the acceleration of electric traction over a given time. At the time - 1901/1902 - the Great Eastern Railway was under pressure from its competitors for the ever-growing volume of commuter traffic to and from the eastern suburbs and there was a danger that these competitors might well have considered electrification. Financially, the Great Eastern was in no position to consider tangling with the infant electrification, hence Holden's mandate from his Directors - a steam locomotive that would accelerate a 300 ton train from rest to 30 mph in 30 seconds. It had, of necessity, to have three cylinders - providing it with two of sufficient power output would have called for a boiler of a higher pressure than the design team cared to contemplate or that the technology of the time could produce. This might well have been the reason why three-cylinder propulsion was not popular - a matter of technology.

Following some modifications, including the raising of the boiler pressure from 200 to 250 psi, the 'Decapod' proved its point, provided the requisite acceleration figures, went into the works at Stratford East whence it emerged in

'X' class 4-8-0T (later LNER class 'T1') No. 1354.   *John Alsop Collection*

an entirely different guise as an 0-8-0 tender engine. From 1902 not much was heard of three-cylinder propulsion until 1907 when it arose, Phoenix-like, and from then until the introduction of British Railways standard locomotives, it never lost its place as the principal means of express locomotive propulsion in the UK. No doubt the afficianados of Stanier and Churchward will be quick to point out that numbers of four-cylinder express locomotives were built - the LMS had 52 including the solitary 'Claughton', the GWR a total of 209 'Stars', 'Castles' and 'Kings', the Southern under Maunsell one class only - the 'Lord Nelsons' - 16 in all, whereas Gresley would have none of it and kept to two or three cylinders and it is a three-cylinder simple locomotive that holds the world speed record for steam traction, not a much vaunted Chapelon four-cylinder compound nor yet a four-cylinder simple.

The rise of three cylinders was helped - indirectly - by Sam Fay, General Manager of the Great Central, Alexander Henderson, Chairman of the company and ultimately by J.G. Robinson. In 1905 the Directors of the GCR under Henderson and aided and abetted by Sam Fay authorized the construction of a gravitational shunting yard at Wath-on-Dearne near Barnsley in South Yorkshire. Known locally as 'Wath hump' it cost the company £190,000 and was designed to cope with the tremendous volume of coal traffic from the local coalfields and handled by the GCR. Trains of 50 wagons or more were assembled and dispatched to various destinations and in order to cope with this traffic, J.G. Robinson was called upon to design a locomotive specifically for the task. He introduced his 'S1' class 'Wath Tanks'. Four were built and they were unusual in that they had three cylinders and had the rarely used 0-8-4 wheel arrangement. It is possible that he was influenced by Holden but it is more than likely that Robinson was concerned with smooth torque and maximum power output at low speeds - after all these 'hump shunters' were to spend their working lives moving slowly and gently around the yard. He used existing components including the Atlantic boiler and outside cylinders, the inside cylinder from the 0-6-0 (LNER 'J11' class) and the coupled wheels and rods from his 0-8-0s. The result was a class of very powerful locomotives that went on forever. They passed into LNER ownership and Gresley was sufficiently interested to rebuild one of them - No. 6171- with a superheater and a booster. The latter is an auxiliary steam engine that in the case of 6171 was coupled to the bogie and helped by supplying extra power when starting.

The hump shunting yard at Newport, Middlesbrough, was situated between the Darlington-Saltburn line and the River Tees. It was a concentration yard for coal from the Durham / Northumberland coalfield, other goods and materials for export from Middlesbrough and for raw materials for the industry of Teesside.

Worsdell - or someone - must, on one occasion, have looked south and taken note of the sterling work being performed by the Robinson hump shunters at Wath and decided that here what was wanted for the Newport Yard. For obvious reasons any engine designed for work in the yard could not be identical with anything produced by the GCR for the same purpose. Having received authorization in July 1908 to build 10 4-8-0s, to their respective drawing boards went members of the design team.

The Wilson Worsdell's 'X' class (LNER 'T1') was a three-cylinder locomotive with the three cylinders, valve chests and smoke box saddle incorporated in one casting. The drive was divided between the leading coupled axle and the second pair of coupled wheels. Three cylinders and divided drive were a first for the NER as was the monobloc casting. Digressing for a moment, it is said that coming events cast their shadows before them - Raven became an enthusiast for three-cylinder propulsion and monobloc casting for the three cylinders; Gresley was similarly keen on three cylinders in one casting although he favoured all cylinders driving onto one axle and Edward Thompson, who moved to Gateshead from Hull in 1909 was fanatical about divided drive. Quite obviously Raven was influenced by Worsdell who, as is mentioned elsewhere, became a champion of three cylinders. Thompson had been with the NER since 1906 working firstly under Bill Farrow at Hull and then under Charlie Baister at Gateshead. Thus, would Thompson be *au fait* with the development of the 'X' class.

Members of the class were thoroughly tested on 1,000 ton trains between Newcastle and Morpeth and between Hull and Bridlington, not that they were ever called upon to carry out such duties. They were allocated to Newport Yard (Middlesbrough) and to Hull and two found their way to March in LNER days. The class was employed on shunting duties at the three yards. The NER engines were the last to be built at Gateshead although five were built by the LNER. Withdrawals began in 1937 with Nos. 1355 and 1358 - the engines that had been transferred to March - being the first to go to the scrapyard. In 1944 eight were still hard at work and the class did not become extinct until No. 1659 (BR 69921) was withdrawn from Consett in June 1961.

The 4-8-0T as class 'T1' in BR days. No. 69915 had been built at Gateshead in 1909 and is photographed on shed at Tees (Newport) Yard.   *John Clewley*

'Y' class 4-6-2T No. 1175, later LNER class 'A7'.   *John Alsop Collection*

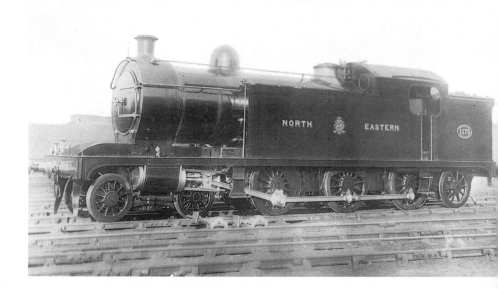

4-6-2 tank originally ordered by Wilson Worsdell in February 1910

The original order was cancelled but re-instated by Raven in November 1910 although the first of the class, No. 1113, was turned out from Darlington works in October 1910. There must have been a breakdown in communication somewhere! There is no evidence that Raven modified the design and the question arises whether or not the 'Y' class 4-6-2T was Raven or Worsdell, the debate continues.

The success of the 'X' class prompted the development of the 'Y' class, locomotives that would be out on the road rather than on mundane shunting duties, able to run fast bunker - first over short distances and capable of hauling trains of 1,000 tons at 20 mph on level track. It is not known whether or not the 'Ys' were ever called upon to emulate this feat but it is recorded that 1126 was put through its paces. It slipped badly whilst hauling 864 tons on a 1 in 185 gradient near Shildon. This emphasised the need for efficient sanding and the class was subsequently fitted with Downs sanding gear. As further additions were not made to the original 20 this implies that there was a weakness somewhere, probably in the area of braking capacity when handling loose-coupled trains.

The 'Ys' were, as with nearly all Raven designs, handsome locomotives and were fitted with Ramsbottom safety valves concealed by a brass trumpet. These were removed from No. 1182 and replaced by Ross pop valves when it disgraced itself by dropping both lead plugs. On reflection, it was the fireman who disgraced himself by allowing the water level to fall below the firebox crown.

As built, the 'Ys' were unsuperheated and a programme of superheating was begun in 1917. Throughout their working lives various modifications were carried out ranging from the standardisation of boilers to the fitting of steam brakes to the bogies on some members of the class. They were allocated throughout the system from Shildon to Leeds and from Starbeck to Percy Main. Withdrawals began in 1951 and the class became extinct with the demise of No. 1191 (BR 69786) in December 1957.

The Pacifics

It is rumoured that when in 1915 G.J. Churchward learnt that Gresley had a 4-6-2 design on the drawing board at Doncaster he commented 'Why is that young man bothering to design a Pacific – we could sell him ours'.

This was, of course, a reference to Churchward's 4-6-2 *The Great Bear* introduced in 1908 and the country's first Pacific. Incidentally, Gresley's 1915 design for a four-cylinder 4-6-2 was shelved and seven years were to pass before the appearance of No. 1470, a three-cylinder Pacific, from Doncaster works.

Raven returned to Darlington in 1919 as Sir Vincent Raven KBE. A grateful country had rewarded him for his war service and a grateful company lost no time in following suit. From the NER minutes, 7th February, 1919, minute No. 12149:

Boiler of unidentified Pacific at Darlington works.   *Doug Hardy*

A view of the frames of an unidentified Pacific with the boiler on the adjacent road.
                    P.N. Townend Collection

Frames of Pacific No. 2400 (later *City of Newcastle*) at Darlington works in 1922. *Doug Hardy*

Monobloc casting of cylinders and valve chest of one of the Pacifics lined up on the cylinder borer at Darlington works. *Doug Hardy*

An unidentified Pacific under construction. The right-hand cylinder and smokebox saddle are clearly visible.   *P.N. Townend Collection*

Raven Pacific No. 2400 at Darlington works.   *Northern Steam Photographs, Darlington*

In view of the fact that Sir Vincent Raven has received no bonus or advance of salary during the war and has been put to considerable expenses in connection with his residence in London since 1915 during the time that he was working at the Ministry of Munitions and at the Admiralty - resolved that a special grant of £2000 be made.

Signed - Knaresborough -Chairman

This equates to £55,000 at 2002 values and at the time that this award was made, Raven's salary was £3,000 pa.

Within a short time of his return to work, Raven produced his mixed traffic 4-6-0, the 'S3' class. This is regarded as an excellent design and it is a great pity that he followed it with what was arguably his nadir - the Pacifics. The Railways Act of 1921 provides something of a clue insofar as the amalgamation of the Country's railways into the 'Big Four' was due to become law on 1st January, 1923 at which time the North Eastern Railway would be absorbed into the London & North Eastern Railway. The NER was the largest and richest of the constituent companies and it had, for instance, a locomotive stud of 2,001 as against the Great Central Railway - 1,361 and the Great Northern - 1,359.

The introduction of the Pacifics by Raven has been the cause of much speculation by successive generations of railway writers. Some are of the opinion that the NER Directors used them as a diversionary tactic to take Raven's mind off electrification; others that the Directors were looking to the time when the East Coast route would be LNER and that when this occurred the former North Eastern Railway would be able to contribute a class of locomotive capable of handling prestige expresses from King's Cross to Edinburgh.

Authorization for the construction of two Pacifics is dated 30th March, 1922, although according to the late Ken Hoole the order for the first two was placed at Darlington works on 26th January, 1921. As it was November 1922 before the first was ex-works, it seems that there wasn't such a rush to complete the engines as we have been led to believe. Nevertheless, so enthusiastic were the Directors that details of the locomotives were released to the press well before they were completed and there is little doubt that company prestige was involved. In the meantime, Gresley had stolen a march and, in 1922, introduced his Pacifics from an entirely new design - and that is a very important point. The history of the steam locomotive in this country is studded with classes of locomotives that have not only been quite outstanding as working units but have added lustre to railway operation. From Stephenson's long-boilered goods to Gresley's 'A4' class they have one common factor - they were built to new designs. When a new class was introduced as a modification of an existing design, the result has not always been a happy one. Churchward took his 'Star' class design and 'stretched' it and the resultant *The Great Bear* is regarded as a Churchward failure. Incidentally, there is no record of Churchward's comments on hearing of Raven's Pacifics.

The NER had no more use for a Pacific than had the GWR some 14 years before and this is crystallised superbly in some lines from Dr W.A. Tuplin's *North Eastern Steam*. They are taken from a section headed 'Not So Pacific'.

When somebody told you (said the driver) that they were building new engines nearly twice as big as a 'Z' you didn't know what to think about it. A 'Z' could take eighteen coaches from York to Darlington in 50 minutes so what more did they want? Did they want to do it in forty minutes or did they want to run thirty coach trains? And did they think that a bigger engine was bound to be better than a 'Z'? You could kill a fireman on a 'Z' if you thrashed her for half an hour so what's the good of building anything bigger? They built an electric engine for expresses between York and Newcastle but they never put any wires up to run it with. Did they know what they were doing with their Pacifics or whatever they called them? One of my mates said he'd heard that the Great Northern had built a couple of Pacifics and that our lot were doing the same just to stop the Great Northern being one up on us. Well you wouldn't think that they would be such big kids as that, but then you never know. First an electric with no electricity to run it and then a monster that's sure to be too long for some of the curves. They go out of their way to look for trouble as if it didn't come fast enough on its own. Always playing about with something different and just beating themselves with it. Look at the 'S' they fitted with cylinders nearly as big as the boiler. The Stump they called it, or something like that, never any good. They always have to be making things bigger and they get worse every time. [The driver continues:] We heard that at Darlington they were rushing the new engines a bit so as to get one or two out before the end of the year (1922). They managed it and rumours came round of an engine on eighteen wheels and as long as the biggest coaches. Nobody believed that and presently the news came that it was the engine and tender that had eighteen wheels between them. The engine, they said, was like a long fat 'Z' with a firebox about twice as wide as on the 'Z'. It had six driving wheels and three cylinders. Pity they couldn't work a few more in while they were at it.

As with the 'Z' class Atlantics, the NER Pacifics had three cylinders in line with piston valve chests integral in a casting that supported the smokebox and the cylinders drove onto the leading pair of coupled wheels. One of Raven's draughtsmen, Dick Innes, records in his diary that he pointed out to Raven that the Pacific was a long engine and that if the drive was to the first pair of coupled wheels it would be even longer. It seems that Raven did not take too kindly to the observation, lost his temper, banged his desk and shouted 'I have always driven onto the leading coupled axle and I am going to with the Pacific'. What he chose to ignore was that six eccentrics and the middle big end had to be accommodated on the crank axle, a similar arrangement as on the Atlantics. The *NER Magazine* for August 1922 gives details as follows:

New 4-6-2 locomotive now under construction at Darlington to the designs of Sir Vincent Litchfield Raven, K.B.E., M.I.C.E., M.I. Mec.E.

3 cylinders 19 in. x 26 in. cylinders and steam chest in one casting.
Steam chest common to all cylinders. Three exhaust pipes unite at the bottom of a single blast pipe.
Piston valves 8¾ in. diameter, actuated by Stephenson link motion.

Driving wheels	6 ft 8 in.
Rigid wheelbase	15 ft 0 in.
Total wheelbase	37 ft 2 in.
Bogie wheel diameter	3 ft 1 in.
Bogie wheel wheelbase	6 ft 6 in.
Trailing wheelbase	3 ft 9 in.
Trailing wheel sideplay	31 in.
Distance between tubeplates	21 ft 0 in.
Boiler diameter (plates)	6 ft 0 in.

Boiler diameter with cladding	6 ft 3 in.
Tubes 118	2 in. diameter
Flues 24	5 in.
Firebox length	8 ft 0 in.
Smokebox diameter	6 ft 5 in.
Grate area	41 sq. feet
Tender water capacity	4,125 gallons
Tender coal capacity	5½ tons
Overall length loco and tender	72 ft 4 in.
Adhesion weight	60 tons
Engine and tender weight	143 tons 2 cwt
Pressure	200 psi

The first, No. 2400, was completed in November 1922 and entered traffic the following month. The second, No. 2401, was included on the stock list at 31st December, 1922 and entered traffic on 9th January, 1923. From the *NER Magazine* for February a photograph of No. 2400 *City of Newcastle* with the caption 'This engine is exciting interest wherever it goes - the largest passenger engine in Britain'. There is an element of licence here as No. 2400 hadn't been very far when the photograph was published and the implication is that big is beautiful. Raven's Pacifics were certainly big but fell short of Ivatt's dictum 'if a locomotive looks good, it is good'.

When No. 2400 was outshopped, Raven sent Tom Blades, doyen of the Gateshead drivers, to Darlington to bring her home. On arrival at Gateshead, Raven fussed around his creation and enquired of Blades what he thought of the locomotive. Raven was somewhat disgruntled with a less than enthusiastic reply. Blades told Raven in no uncertain Tyneside terms that he would have trouble with the 'inside bearants' on the pony truck. When Raven enquired why this should be so, Blades replied, 'Why man, for wan thing thems te neor the fayer'. (The bearings are too close to the firebox.) And indeed, Blades was proved to be correct and the three members of the class that were built in 1924 were fitted with Cartazzi sliding axle boxes to the pony truck.

On 1st January, 1923 the LNER came into being, Sir Vincent Raven retired and Nos. 2400 and 2401 passed into the ownership of the new company with GNR Pacifics Nos. 1470 and 1471 as stablemates. On 3rd September, 1922, Gresley arranged a test run from King's Cross to Grantham and back with Nos. 1470 and 1471 hauling 600 ton trains and sporting the indicator shelter. So impressed with their respective performances were the Directors that an order was placed for a further 10 Pacifics. The first of the batch was No. 4472 *Flying Scotsman* entering service in January 1923 and the tenth was No. 4481 *St. Simon*, leaving the works in August 1923. There were now 12 Gresley Pacifics and two Raven Pacifics on the strength and it would have been easy for Gresley to abandon Nos. 2400 and 2401 and use his design as standard but he was nothing if not open-minded and initiated comparative trials.

The locomotives chosen were No. 2400 *City of Newcastle* and the third GNR Pacific No. 1472 - (LNER 4472 *Flying Scotsman*). To emphasise the 'fairness' of the trials, Gresley used the NER dynamometer car and crew and chose the hardest 'turns' on the timetable at that time - the 10.51 am Doncaster-King's Cross and the return working at 5.40 pm. The issue was not in doubt even with

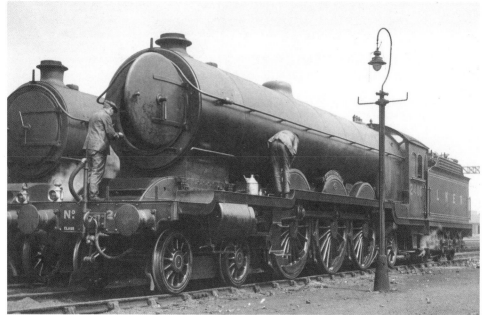

Raven Pacific No. 2400 *City of Newcastle* receiving attention. The presence of the oil can near the smokebox saddle suggests that the footplate crew is preparing the locomotive for a spell of duty.
P.N. Townend Collection

No. 2403 *City of Durham* at York station.   *P.N. Townend Collection*

Tom Blades at the regulator of No. 2400. As the figures confirmed, 2400 consumed coal at the rate of 58.7 lb. per mile, water at the rate of 40.4 gallons per mile and produced 875 drawbar horse power. The figures for No. 4472 are 52.6 lb. per mile, 38.3 gallons per mile and 928 drawbar horse power. The outcome of the trials was an order for a further 40 Gresley Pacifics.

So what of Raven's Pacifics? Three more were delivered in 1924 and between then and 1929 the class worked between York and Newcastle. In 1929 and in an attempt to improve the steaming, No. 2404 *City of Ripon* was rebuilt with a standard LNER 'A1' boiler. As there was little improvement in performance, rebuilding of its classmates could not be justified. In any case, rebuilding of the front end to comply with the Gresley 'A1' front end would have been prohibitively expensive. The class as a whole underwent several modifications during its short life. The effective heating surface of the boilers was increased in 1933; the steam reversing gear that was fitted when the locomotives were new had a penchant for creeping into full forward mode when running with adverse effects on the fire and the fireman and was replaced by screw-operated gear; bronze driving axle boxes replaced the steel variety in 1929 and there was chopping and changing of brake equipment between 1931 and 1935. Additionally, the axle boxes and bearings ran hot - a weekly occurrence which was in some measure due to the inaccessibility of some of the oiling points. Perhaps the most surprising modification was the fitting of chrome nickel alloy steel coupling and connecting rods to three of the class shortly before they were withdrawn.

Thus was the class consigned to perdition and transferred from Gateshead to York in 1934 - the year that Raven died - and as and when heavy repairs became due, the locomotives were scrapped.

Few records of the performance of the Pacifics exist apart from tests carried out officially - amateur observers of the time do not seem to have been interested in them. In *British Pacific Locomotives* C.J. Allen touches on a run from Darlington to York behind No. 2402 *City of York* and notes that it touched 80 mph at Alne. He is then somewhat dismissive of the performance by stating that the load was only 245 tons. Similarly, O.S. Nock records a run behind No. 2401 *City of Kingston-upon-Hull* on the up 'Flying Scotsman' when it touched 72 mph at Beal. He goes on to observe that a 'Z' class Atlantic could have done equally well 'if put to it'.

In Peter Townend's *East Coast Pacifics at Work* E.L. Bell advances the theory that the indifferent performances of the locomotives is attributable to indifferent driving and he names the drivers and comments on their respective attitudes. He says, for instance that 'Blades could be an enterprising driver when he chose as he showed in the trials against the GN Pacific but he chose very seldom in ordinary running'. Bell continues, 'The engines therefore got little encouragement from the drivers except for Knight so their day to day performance was mediocre and rightfully described as no better than a good "Z"'.

In the November 2002 issue of the *Northern Eastern Express* George Hearse writes, 'When I was in the Locomotive Drawing Office at Darlington there were two subjects it was wise not to raise, one was Edward Thompson and the other

No. 2404 *City of Ripon* before modification. Apart from the Cartazzi axleboxes, the photograph shows the locomotive as built. Note the cab just visible at the left of the picture. It is probably of a class 'D' two-cylinder compound equipped with Smith's piston valves or a class 'G' 2-4-0 introduced in 1887 and known as 'Waterburys'.   *P.N. Townend Collection*

No. 2404 *City of Ripon*, note the modifications: new boiler, Gresley cab, pony truck fitted with Cartazzi axleboxes and an LNER tender.   *P.N. Townend Collection*

was the North Eastern Pacific locomotives'. According to the article (that makes much of the opinions of the late Dick Inness), the trouble with the Pacifics is that they were North Eastern, designed by Raven and built at Darlington and that 'unfair Doncaster criticism tarnished their image'. But indicator shelter and dynamometer car results would show otherwise. It should not be forgotten that three of the Pacifics were built after the Grouping - had Gresley wished he could no doubt have put forward a strong case for cancelling the order.

Raven's Pacifics were unique in the context of the NER and giving them names added to their 'uniqueness' - the only class of NER locomotives thus dignified - the purists will, of course, argue that only Nos. 2400/1 were named under the aegis of the NER whereas Nos. 2402/2404 were named after the Grouping. Wholesale naming of locomotives was a post-Grouping phenomenon when each of the companies went for naming in a big way. The LMS appealed to our jingoism and further edified the travelling public with a spot of Greek Mythology; the SR involved the travelling public in Arthurian legend; the LNER appealed to man's sporting instincts in naming its Pacifics after famous racehorses and as for the Great Western anything painted green was named, however inappropriately, from *Tre Pol and Pen* to *Blasius*.

The accompanying table gives the building, transfer and withdrawal dates of the NER Pacifics and when viewed as a collection shows that the names were not very imaginative. There are apocryphal stories of gullible travellers assuming that if the train engine was, say, *City of Newcastle* that was the destination of the train. Nevertheless, in naming the Pacifics the NER was in the vanguard of the concept of naming whole classes of locomotives and that is, perhaps, a fitting epitaph.

No.	Built	Name	To York	Withdrawn
2400	12/22	City of Newcastle	7th May 1934	April 1937
2401	12/22	City of Kingston-upon-Hull	9th Feb. 1934	July 1936
2402	3/24	City of York	13th August 1934	July 1936
2403	3/24	City of Durham	26th April 1934	May 1937
2404	3/24	City of Ripon	7th Nov. 1934	Feb. 1937

It is a great pity that Raven's Pacific design was, compared with the 'S' and 'Z' classes, a failure and a less than happy finale to a career that if not star-studded was certainly distinguished.

In *The Hollow Man* T.S. Eliot writes, 'This is the way that the world ends - not with a bang but with a whimper' and in relation to the Pacifics the quotation is appropriate.

Portrait of Vincent Raven. *LNER*

Portrait of A.C. Stamer. *LNER* Portrait of Eric Geddes.

Chapter Nine

Raven, the NER and World War I

Raven's secondment to Woolwich Arsenal dated from 15th September, 1915. It came at the behest of Lloyd George, the then Minister of Munitions in Asquith's coalition government. Sir Frederick Donaldson who was in charge of Woolwich at the beginning of the war was sent to America and Canada to organize vital supplies and this left a vacancy and that vacancy was filled by Raven. But why Raven? He had been CME for five years and had made positive contributions to those sections of the NER for which he was responsible. The declaration of war and all that that implied for the company would have kept him busy but Eric Geddes, who was made Deputy Director General of Munitions in May 1915 and was aware of Raven's abilities, might well have recommended him to Lloyd George. Is it, therefore, coincidence that Raven's secondment followed hard on the heels of Geddes'? In addition, in the summer of 1915 Field Marshall Lord Kitchener alerted the Government to the fact that he was concerned about the delivery of munitions to the troops on the Western Front. He said that it was slow and he attributed this to drunkenness - which was commonplace - amongst the munitions workers. Lloyd George conceded that alcohol was a problem and went so far as to comment that the Country's enemies were Germany, Austria and alcohol. Thus, a strong hand was needed at Woolwich and the powers-that-be decided that Raven was the man. This decision could well have been influenced by the fact that Raven had an extremely capable deputy in A.C. Stamer, Raven's right-hand man and one of the unsung heroes of the development of the NER.

Arthur Cowie Stamer, born in March 1869, was the fifth son of the Bishop Suffragan of Shrewsbury, the Rt Revd Sir L.L. Stamer, another coincidental link between the railway and the Church. Educated at Rugby, he served a pupil apprenticeship with Beyer, Peacock in Manchester before joining the NER. His career pattern was always one step behind that of Raven and he became Gresley's principal assistant on the formation of the LNER. Stamer was President of the Institute of Locomotive Engineers in 1923. He retired in 1933 and died exactly 10 years to the day - 14th February, 1944 - as Raven. Military in bearing, an enthusiastic sportsman and with an urbane personality he was well-liked by the workforce and was most certainly the man capable of ensuring the smooth running of the works for which he assumed responsibility.

Some idea of the esteem in which Arthur Stamer was held may be gauged from the events that were organised to mark his retirement in 1933. On 14th December, 300 members of the CME's department, past and present, gathered at Houndgate Hall, Darlington and during the course of the evening, Gresley made presentations of a canteen of cutlery and a notoring bag and paid tribute to the 'loyal and valauble service that he had received from Mr Stamer'. The photograph shows the principal guests.

This was followed on 29th December, 1933 with a dinner at the Royal Station Hotel when Stamer was entertained by officers of the North Eastern Area. His personality was summed up with a paraphrase of the words of W.S. Gilbert:

Among the four bowler-hatted gentleman near Wilson Worsdell 'S1' class 4-6-0 No. 2115 is A.C. Stamer, second from left and partially obscured.   *Doug Hardy*

Below left: A poor quality image which shows a group photograph at the occasion of the presentation made to A.C. Stamer at Houndgate Hall, Darlington on 14th December, 1933. Front row are (*from left to right*): E. Thompson. L. Farr, A.C. Stamer, H.N. Gresley, and P. Liddell. Those in the back row include, E. Stephenson, H. Oxtoby, W. Wells Hood, Mr Page, Mr Turner, Mr Carr, Mr Drury and Mr Greenside.

Below right: Portrait of J.H. Smeddle.   *LNER*

His heart was twice as good as gold and twenty times as mellow.
Good temper triumphed in his face and in his face and in his heart he held a place for
All the erring human race and every wretched fellow.*

Following the dinner there were presentations - a radiogram and an antique writing desk - and Gresley saying more or less what he had said on the 14th December. Other speakers included Jenkin Jones, J.H. Smeddle and H.A. Watson. But of all the tributes he received, it is thought that Stamer was most proud of those paid to him by the AEU, the Boilermakers' Society, Faverdale Branch, and the Gateshead Shopmen's branch of the NUR. In presenting Stamer with a chiming clock J.T. Dixon of the AEU said that it was the first time in his life that he had known the trade unions hold such a function. Mr Stamer had been their chief during 10 of the most difficult years within memory and had always shown regard for the men's point of view.

A contributor to the *LNER Magazine* wrote,

> A man whose word was his bond, a tireless worker trusted and respected by all the thousands of workmen he has controlled [and continues] he takes with him into retirement the sincerest wishes of the whole of his staff that he will retain his present good health for many years so that he may enjoy the outdoor pursuits of which he is so fond.

There were other gatherings and tributes but there was no reference to Raven amongst them. Stamer's career was carefully reviewed from joining Beyer, Peacock to retiring and in reply to one speech he commented that he had been fortunate in having Gresley as his chief for 10 years. One is left to wonder about Stamer's omission of Raven. Was he not well enough to attend - remember that the celebrations were only weeks before Raven's death - was he invited and declined? As we have seen there are unanswered questions hanging over Raven's life. Is this one more?

Thus, Raven went off to Woolwich as Acting Chief Superintendent and Stamer took over at Darlington as Acting CME. Within three months of Raven's arrival at Woolwich, Lloyd George reported, in glowing terms, to the House of Commons on the changes that Raven had implemented. The Minister instanced a 60-80 per cent increase in the manufacture and filling of certain items with only a 23 per cent increase in staff. He also praised Raven's introduction of statistical analysis. What he didn't mention was that amongst those un-named items were smoke cones for the Gallipoli campaign, the maintenance of boot repairing machinery for Salonika and hay pressing machinery for the Serbian government. In November 1915 Winston Churchill resigned from the cabinet over the Gallipoli debacle.

One problem that Raven had to tackle as a result of the increase in productivity was the storage of explosives. This was solved by using caves at Chislehurst. Electricity was installed and the caves were given a new lease of life. They were used for storage again during World War II and, the war having ended, they became the venue of Rock concerts long before Glastonbury was invented.

There might have been a hidden agenda in appointing Raven to Woolwich. The Arsenal covered some 1,350 acres and had 150 miles of internal railway of mixed gauge serviced by 110 locomotives and 2,000-plus items of rolling stock. This was not the best maintained system in the world and the increase of traffic as a result of the war brought with it congestion and derailments were frequent, so much so

* In the report of the evening's proceedings, this quote was wrongly stated to be from *Iolanthe*, it is, in fact, from *The Gondoliers*.

that breakdown gangs were available 24 hours a day throughout the war. There is no direct evidence that Raven was involved in the maintenance of the Woolwich railway system but it is recorded that four standard gauge locomotives were converted from coal fired to oil fired as the supply of coal, not only for the railway but also for the production of gas and electricity, was a cause of anxiety and it is also recorded that in March 1916 the system was 'standardized'. What exactly was meant by standardized is not revealed although it is safe to assume that it refers to the gauge and that any remaining narrow gauge track was scrapped. Another interesting note records that in order to cope with the demand on goods wagons, 50 were hired at a cost of 6s. per wagon per week reducing to 5s. per wagon per week from - surprise - the North Eastern Railway!

Following the attack on Hartlepool by a German warship, there was an ever-present threat of German naval activity in the North Sea curtailing coal traffic from the North East and meeting the demand by rail would have been both difficult and costly. To overcome this, coal was obtained from the Kent coalfield and even so, supplies became dangerously low. Received information is that at times of war the country is unified, everyone faces the same way, we all pull together and that industrial unrest and strikes are unthinkable. The reality is different and strikes were not unknown in either the 1914-18 or 1939-45 conflicts. For instance, in 1915 there were two serious strikes - munition workers in Scotland and miners in England. Raven might have been forgiven for thinking that he had left his labour and staffing problems in the North East but there were difficulties in maintaining manning levels at Woolwich throughout the war. This instability was brought about by staff leaving for better jobs or joining the services. In addition there were strikes of power station workers, engine drivers and firemen in 1917 and again in 1918. Nationally, 5.5 million working days were lost in 1918 and the civilian population was in a ferment over the shortage of food. There were food riots and in two Durham villages children died of starvation. Eventually, in the Spring of 1918 the Government introduced food rationing. This was the background against which Raven had to ensure the continuing production of armaments and cope with some of the irritations outlined. Whilst at Woolwich and with the Admiralty, Raven had made a contribution - consciously or unconsciously - as the methods that he introduced and that influenced production were developed and thus formed the basis for weapons and armaments production between the wars.

In the meantime, Geddes was as active as ever. In August 1916 he went to France to organize transport, especially the efficient use of standard gauge railway, becoming Field Marshal Haig's Inspector General of Transport. Edward Thompson, Raven's son-in-law who was with the GNR at Doncaster, was seconded to Woolwich although he did not stay long before joining the staff of the Director General of Transportation in France who was, of course, Geddes. To complete 1916, it was the first year of British Summer Time, the first battle of the Somme during which there were 20,000 casualties in the first hour, Asquith, the Prime Minister was ousted and was succeeded by Lloyd George.

The year 1917 saw another career move for Geddes when he went to the Admiralty - later becoming First Lord - and in the same year, Raven became in turn Deputy Controller of Armament Production for the Admiralty and in Autumn 1917, Controller answering directly to Vice-Admiral Sir Eric Geddes.

Also in 1917 King George V instituted the Most Excellent Order of the British Empire and Raven was appointed Knight Commander of the Order in recognition of his war work, thus becoming Sir Vincent.

Meanwhile, back at Darlington, Stamer was coping not only with the construction of locomotives and rolling stock but also with essential war work being carried out at North Road and Shildon. The Darlington National Projectile Factory was built at Government expense and opened in 1915. It was managed by the NER and it was agreed that when the war ended it would be taken over by the company together with the relevant plant and machinery. The factory was staffed by 1,000 women and girls and they turned out over one and a half million shells in the course of the war. Additionally, the locomotive stock had to be maintained and, not surprisingly, the output of new locomotives was reduced. In 1915 12 'Z' class 4-4-2s were built; in 1916 two 'Zs'; 1917 20 'T2' 0-8-0s and four 'Zs' and in 1917 20 'T2s' and one 'Z' class. If this wasn't sufficient for Stamer he became involved with extra meat rations for manual workers, the problems of employing aliens and 'the release of lads to the Colours'. He was also responsible for the rehabilitation of disabled employees and he argued, successfully, for 11 categories ranging from former employees who had been wounded and subsequently invalided out of the services to the widows and/or dependants of former employees who had been killed on active service and were deemed to be 'in necessitous circumstances'. Stamer followed this up with a list of no fewer than 59 jobs defined as 'light' work ranging from muniment room attendant to the not quite so exotic lavatory attendant and some 500 people took advantage of the scheme.

During the course of war, 34 per cent of the workforce joined the armed services and, as a result, women were recruited to fill the vacancies and were employed throughout the system in jobs as diverse as engine cleaning and crane driving. They were not allowed on the footplate under any circumstances and there is at least one example of a female being dismissed for transgressing the rule. They had to produce a brass token or check when reporting for work and collect it as they went home. This enabled the timekeepers to know whether or not the women were at work and for how long. The conditions were Draconian - if a check was lost a penny fine was imposed for a new check and should a female cleaner be 15 minutes late in reporting for work, she lost half-an-hour's pay and should she be more than 15 minutes late she was sent home and lost a day's pay.

Coincidentally, Raven had women on his workforce at Woolwich where they undertook dangerous and exacting jobs such as the manufacturing and filling of shells. It was discovered that women were just as efficient as men in whatever work they undertook and, in some cases, better and they did not spend as much of their wages on drink as did men. The drink problem amongst men gave rise to concern throughout the war years to such an extent that the Government sought to limit opening hours and increased the price of beer. Those who were engaged on munitions work had, however, greater hazards to face than 'the evils of drink'. Prolonged working with TNT gave a yellowish tinge to the skin and the women were known as 'canaries'. In addition they suffered from respiratory problems, skin disorders and the dangers associated with explosives. It is estimated that between 1915 and 1918 a million women entered paid employment for the first time and 800,000 of them were engaged in the engineering and munitions industries. Raven kept his finger on the pulse of Darlington and travelled to his home as often as possible. It takes little imagination to visualize Stamer and the Chief swapping notes on their respective female work forces. The Fourth Reform Act of 1918 giving women over 30 the vote and the Sex Disqualification (Removal) Act 1919 changed the status of women for good.

The NER Directors were not happy about employees who joined up without permission and made their feelings known. It seems that although the company was obliged to re-instate them on their return from the services, there was to be a certain show of reluctance which Stamer was expected to implement.

The war over, the servicemen were demobilized, returned to Lloyd George's land fit for heroes and the female employees were summarily dismissed. Sadly, 2,236 NER employees did not return and their names are inscribed on the War Memorial that stands in York in the shadow of the City walls and opposite the former NER offices. The memorial, designed by Sir Edwin Lutyens, was dedicated by the Archbishop of York in the presence of - amongst others - Field Marshal Lord Plumer, Sir Charles Harrington, C-in-C Northern Command, and Lord Knaresborough, formerly Chairman, NER.

It was not uncommon for battalions to be formed from volunteers from the same district - the Accrington Pals and the Barnsley Pals are examples. At the instigation of Sir Eric Geddes the NER Battalion was raised during the early days of the war and writing in 1925 he observed,

> The NER Battalion, formed in the first days of the war is, I think, unique in being the only complete battalion raised out of the employees of one Company - an origin that it maintained throughout the war.

Geddes's initiative was supported by the NER insofar as the company undertook to make provision for dependent relatives with respect to housing, job security and pensions. From the enlisting of the first recruit to the battalion being fully equipped took a mere 80 days. Much to Geddes' chagrin, the battalion was not attached to the Royal Engineers but was styled the 17th Northumberland Fusiliers. It was disbanded in June 1919 and the Colours laid up in the Cathedral Church of St Nicholas, Newcastle-upon-Tyne.

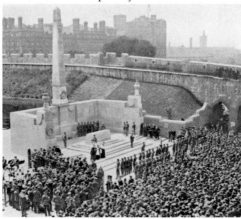

Unveiling of the War Memorial at York.

Chapter Ten

Succession and Retirement

The Act that created the 'Big Four' companies also created an amount of political in-fighting. Although there was tacit agreement that the North Eastern, as the largest of the constituent companies, would provide the Chief General Manager in the person of R.L. Wedgwood, the North British would provide the Chairman, William Whitelaw, and the Great Central the Deputy Chairman, Lord Faringdon, what, however, of the chief mechanical engineer? The front runners were Robinson, Raven and Gresley of whom Gresley was the youngest. Furthermore he had continuous service, his career not having been interrupted by the war whereas Raven had lost nearly four years 'locomotive work' and was, in any case, approaching retirement age but he was - apart from J.G. Robinson who was beyond retirement age - the senior mechanical engineer of all of the constituent companies. Others that might have been in contention were Hill of the GER, Heywood of the Great North of Scotland and Chalmers of the North British.

In the intervening 80-plus years, speculation has been rife and various theories have been advanced and various reasons given as to why the CME's job went to Gresley and not to either Raven or Robinson. The following points are a summary of received information:

a) Having started his career with Edward Fletcher and continued with the NER was Raven considered to lack experience or at least was his experience too narrow to be in charge of locomotive affairs from Scotland to King's Cross?

b) Assuming that Raven was selected and that 65 was the age at which employees retired from service with the LNER then within 18 months the selection process would have to be repeated. This would reduce Raven's tenure of office to the level of an interregnum - not good for stability.

c) By joining the Board of Metropolitan-Vickers in 1922 did Raven imply that he was not interested in the LNER job?

d) Were the Directors of the newly-formed company alarmed at the prospect of electrification raising its head should Raven be appointed?

e) Robinson claimed in a letter to the *Railway Gazette* in May 1941 shortly after Gresley's death that Robinson declined the CME's job and recommended Gresley. The letter deals at some length with the circumstances surrounding the offer and is reproduced in full in David Jackson's excellent biography of Robinson (Oakwood Press). In the final paragraph of the letter Robinson contends that Lord Faringdon expressed disappointment when he declined the appointment and asked him - Robinson - to recommend someone. And that, according to J.G. Robinson is how Gresley came to be appointed. Information recently received however puts a somewhat different slant on the above. It is suggested that Lord Faringdon and William Whitelaw put it gently to Robinson that whilst appreciating his position would it not be in the company's interests for a younger man to be appointed? Robinson conceded and was retained for one year as consultant. It should be remembered that Robinson's letter was written some 18 years after the event and when he was approaching 85 and that the other principal players involved were not available for comment. Perhaps Robinson's memory played him false - it is, after all, but a short step from anecdotage to dotage.

f)   By handing the job to Gresley, the Directors could be satisfied that there should, all things being equal, be a period of stability in locomotive matters of some 15 years. In addition, Gresley had wide experience - Crewe, Horwich and, of course carriage and wagon work with the GNR under H.A. Ivatt. Thus, Gresley's appointment as CME was recommended by the Locomotive Committee on 22nd February, 1922: 'Item 20 - Resolved that it be recommended that Mr H.N. Gresley be appointed Chief Mechanical Engineer of the company at a salary of £4500 pa.' Had the minute been as follows: 'On the recommendation of Mr J.G. Robinson' and so on then this at least would have given credence to Robinson's claims.

Retirement

Raven retired from railway service on 31st December, 1922. In the months preceding Grouping, he had chaired meetings of a committee of the constituent companies' mechanical engineers that concerned itself with, amongst other things, the provision of locomotives, post-Grouping. He had served the North Eastern Railway continuously from 1876 - apart from his secondment to Woolwich - and had had a very successful and fulfilling career. He was a member of several learned societies including the Institutions of Mechanical, Electrical and Civil Engineers and his applications to join these bodies were strongly supported by some of the country's leading engineers.

He was elected an Associate Member of the Institute of Civil Engineers in 1898 proposed by Aspinall of the Lancashire and Yorkshire Railway, H.A. Ivatt of the Great Northern and James Kitson of Kitson and Company. His application for full membership of the Institute was supported by the Worsdells, Lindsay Wood and Oliver Bury amongst others and confirmed in January 1911. He was also elected a member of the North East Coast Institute of Engineers.

The NER was absorbed into the LNER and Raven was retained as Chief Technical Adviser for a year. He was quickly into his new role and he was asked to report on the organization of the LNER's running departments. His submissions are dated 9th February, 1923, thirteen days before the appointment of Gresley was recommended by the Locomotive Committee. It comes as no surprise that Raven had been very thorough in the preparation of the report which is, in itself, a lesson in objectivity. He identifies five methods of organizing locomotive running departments as follows:

1.   All the running shed staffs for both working and repairs under the CME.
2.   A separate Running Superintendent who is independent of the CME and the Operating Department.
3.   All the engine drivers, firemen, cleaners under the Operating Department; the repairs and supervision of locomotives when not working under the CME.
4.   The Operating Department has charge of the running sheds, both working and repairs, and merges the working of the departments into one organisation.
5.   The Running Superintendent holds the position of Assistant to the CME but is responsible to the Superintendent of the Line for locomotive operation. The engine drivers and firemen are under the CME for disciplinary purposes.

He comments in detail on the pros and cons of the above and comes out in favour of 4. He notes that the substance of 3 was tried by one railway - not named in the report - and that it was a failure. He reminds the Board that what works satisfactorily for a small company will not necessarily work 'for so large an undertaking as the London & North Eastern Railway' and hits the Directors with a plethora of statistics:

It must be remembered that the Group has now 7,393 locomotives, 20,275 carriages, 301,354 wagons, a vast amount of machinery at its docks of which there are 38 together with the machinery at the different warehouses and hotels the design and maintenance of which must of necessity be under the CME. These in themselves will require a body of men at present numbering 31,182.

Raven then argues that the CME is responsible for the above and that 'it would be unwise to burden him with the work attached to the running department'.

Not surprisingly in view of his experiences, he recommends that the CME is not involved in conciliation matters noting that:

There has been for some years increasing difficulty in dealing with the running staff [and that] It is undesirable that this work should continue in the CME's department since it would devolve upon him, as the head to give much time and thought to settling questions which could be dealt far more satisfactorily by the Running Superintendent who would devote the whole of his time to this side of the railway.

He comes to the conclusion that the best and most economical system of managing running departments is,

. . . that adopted by the London, Midland and Scottish Railway as it brings full control of the Operating under one head and enables that Department to arrange the engine and train working to fit into the best and most economical advantage, reducing the train and engine mileage per ton of traffic hauled. [and he adds] An organisation of this kind however, largely depends upon its success in having the right personnel in the Departments when changes are made: this is not always possible and from the discussions that have taken place, *I hardly think that they exist on the London and North Eastern Railway* [author's italics].

Raven was present at a meeting of the Locomotive Committee on 12th April, 1923 when the report was discussed and he was also present at the meeting in the following July when it was adopted.

The year 1923 was a particularly busy one for Raven. Apart from the above he also reported on the utilisation of the new company's workshops and he chaired a committee that enquired into the electrification of the former Great Northern Railway's suburban system - the 'Northern Heights' as far as Hitchin. The substance of his report on the workshops was that locomotive construction should be concentrated at Darlington and Doncaster and that construction at Stratford should be phased out. He was in fact quite critical of Stratford averring that engineering practices were outmoded and that as wages and salaries were subject to London weighting, the company was not receiving value for money. He recommended that both Darlington and Doncaster works should be enlarged and that the equipment at Darlington should be updated. The Locomotive Committee accepted Raven's recommendations on Stratford, agreed that Darlington and Doncaster - with a little help from Gorton - could cope with the projected locomotive building programme but did not support his proposals on expansion.

The electrification enquiry was something very close to his heart and he was the obvious choice for Chairman of the committee. Consideration was given to systems operating at pressures of (a) 600 volts DC or (b) 1,500 volts DC with third rail or overhead collection. The committee settled in favour of 1,500 volts DC - which had from a health and safety point of view to be overhead collection - as it was thought that this system would be the more economical especially if main line extension was to be considered. Plans became sufficiently advanced for Raven to contact Metro-Vick, BTH and English Electric with a view to initial tenders for the work. He recommended that should the work go ahead that the traction side and signalling should be separated with a senior engineer in charge of each department but he left the committee, presumably to join Sam Fay's working party to New Zealand. Gresley took over as Chairman from January 1924 but the parlous financial position of the LNER meant that the propositions were doomed from the start. The Board must have been well aware of this and one can only speculate as to why the committee was set up in the first place - was it to ensure that Raven earned his £4,000 Technical Adviser's fee?

In 1924 Raven was a member of a working party headed by Sir Sam Fay, formerly General Manager of the Great Central Railway, that examined and reported on railway workshop practices in New South Wales and New Zealand. It is probable that he was invited to join the working party at the behest of the Governor General of New Zealand, Admiral of the Fleet the Earl Jellicoe, who was well aware of Raven's flair for works organization from his time with the Admiralty. Amongst the recommendations were the replacement of obsolete plant and machinery, the introduction of new training practices and the recruitment of fully qualified engineering staff. The latter comment is thought to have precipitated the early retirement of the chief engineer. Not all of the working party's recommendations were greeted with joy unconfined - its comments on health and safety issues were rejected.

In 1925 Raven was elected President of the Institute of Mechanical Engineers and in his inaugural address he reviewed the development of mechanical engineering from its beginning to its becoming a recognized profession and, in addition, he referred to his visit to New Zealand. The vote of thanks was given by Sir John Aspinall, formerly CME of the Lancashire & Yorkshire Railway. The 1925 summer meeting of the Institute of Mechanical Engineers was held in Newcastle to coincide with the centenary celebrations of the Stockton & Darlington Railway. The keynote speaker was Gresley who delivered a paper on three-cylinder high pressure locomotives during the course of which he complimented Raven on seizing the initiative and introducing three cylinders. Raven told the meeting that he had become a 'convert' as the result of the impression made by the locomotives modified by W.M. Smith. Before calling upon Gresley to reply to some of the comments Raven said that there was a great similarity between his three-cylinder locomotives and those of Gresley with the notable exception of the valve gear. Raven continued, 'So far as that was concerned he always adhered to the Stephenson's valve gear as he believed in simplicity. He used three sets of valve gear and if he went back to railway work to-day he would do the same again'. Gresley, never one to let an opportunity pass, said that he was well aware that Sir Vincent preferred Stephenson's valve gear and that it was obvious that as

Darlington was the home of Stephenson then Stephenson's valve gear should be used there. Raven's vote of thanks was carried with acclamation. In the same year - 1925 - he chaired a committee of technical experts that advised on the reorganization of Indian State Railways. The highlight of the Stockton & Darlington Railway celebrations mentioned above was a parade of locomotives and carriages, 53 exhibits in all, that illustrated the evolution in rail transport from 1825 and each exhibit made its way slowly past the lineside stands that were erected at Fighting Cocks near Darlington. The former North Eastern Railway was represented by No. 1275, Bouch-designed 0-6-0 of 1874; Wilson Worsdell-designed class 'S', 4-6-0 of 1900 LNER No. 2006 (exhibited in Paris in 1900 - *see page 75*); a Fletcher 0-6-0 tank engine; a Wilson Worsdell-designed 'O' class 0-4-4 tank engine No. 1334. Raven was represented by 4-6-2 *City of Newcastle*; 'H' class 4-4-4T No. 2151; one of the Shildon-Newport electric Bo-Bo locomotives preceded by No. 13, the 2-Co-2 electric passenger locomotive that was towed past the admiring audience by T.W. Worsdell-designed 0-6-0 tank engine class 'E' No. 1163; an 'S2' 4-6-0 of 1921, No. 934; three-cylinder 0-8-0 tender engine 'T3' class No. 902 and 'Z1' class Atlantic No. 2207.

A further, if somewhat tenuous link that Raven had with the celebrations is that his former first assistant A.C. Stamer had overall responsibility for the organisation of the parade, ensuring that LNER locomotives were prepared and that representative locomotives from other companies were in the right place at the right time, and at Stockton where the exhibits were shedded prior to leaving for Fighting Cocks, his son-in-law Edward Thompson was in charge. By 1927 Raven had severed all connections with railway work and devoted himself to retirement. Sir Vincent and Lady Raven had always had a strong commitment to the community in the municipality of Darlington and it was rather surprising that they decided to move to Hampshire. They lived for several years at Nately Lodge, Hook, a large house on a two and a half acre site with frontage onto what is now the A30. Sir Vincent followed his interests in shooting and golf and he was also an enthusiastic motorist. Unfortunately, Nately Lodge was destroyed by fire in the 1940s, only the generator house and the stable block being saved. These were converted into a house and the name was retained.

In the autumn of 1933, the Ravens decided to spend the winter at The Felix Hotel, Felixstowe, although one questions the wisdom of exchanging a winter in Hampshire for a winter on the east coast but the golf course at Felixstowe was Sir Vincent's favourite and the hotel was one of a group either managed or owned by the LNER. His health deteriorated early in 1934 and he died from arterial sclerosis on 14th February, aged 75. There were, as was to be expected, obituaries in the professional and technical press and in the local and national press. *The Engineer* was objective in its assessment of Sir Vincent's career and commented: 'Somewhat incisive in manner he was, nevertheless, of a kindly disposition'. The *Northern Dispatch* traced his career and referred to him as a 'vital force in the railway world'. Referring to the 'Railway Race to the North' the same newspaper stated, 'he infused some of his own wonderful energy into the local arrangements for maintaining the velocity of the night express which rushed from London to the North East'. It went on to point out that Mr Raven was on the footplate of the record-breaking locomotive and that it was crewed by Bob Nicholson and Tom Blades. Under the

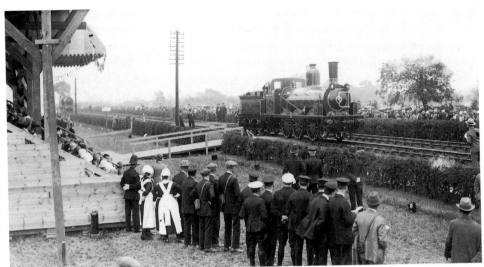

Bouch 0-6-0 No. 1275 built in 1874 passing Cavalcade grandstand at Fighting Cocks near Darlington. The photograph evokes the atmosphere of the Cavalcade - not a bare head in sight and two correctly uniformed nurses on duty but nevertheless taking a great interest in the happenings.
Author's Collection

Former NER 'S' class 4-6-0 No. 2006 photographed prior to taking part in the Centenary Cavalcade. This is the locomotive that was exhibited in Paris in 1900 and was awarded a gold medal. It was the first six-coupled passenger express locomotive to operate on any British railway.
Author's Collection

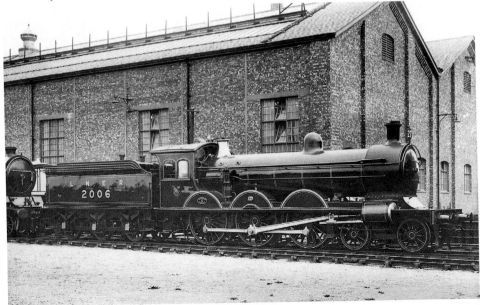

Ex-NER 'D' class 3-cylinder 4-4-4T introduced by Raven in 1913, the class was known as 'Whitby Bogies'. The photograph shows the locomotive in LNER guise as No. 2151 prepared for the 1925 Cavalcade. Between 1931 and 1936 Gresley rebuilt the class as 4-6-2Ts. *Author's Collection*

Ex-North British Railway 3-cylinder (LNER class 'C11') 4-4-2 No. 902 *Highland Chief*. Designed by W.P. Reid, its sister locomotives were modified by Raven at the request of the NBR.

Author's Collection

Mr George Watson with his wife, Mrs Connie Watson. Mrs Watson was Sir Vincent's eldest daughter and was Edward Thompson's sister-in-law. George Watson was Clerk to Darlington Magistrates.

Mrs Anne Hawkins

A photograph taken on 20th January, 1940, the wedding day of George and Connie Watson's son, Michael. *Left to right*: Best Man - Pilot Officer Ernest 'Zeke' Murray, Groom - Pilot Officer Michael Litchfield Watson. PO Watson, who flew Blenheims, was killed in action over Malta in 1941, leaving his wife and seven-month-old baby Anne - now Mrs Anne Hawkins.

Mrs Anne Hawkins

heading 'Men and Affairs' the *Northern Echo* targeted Sir Vincent's implacable opposition to the use of petrol as a means of propulsion for railway locomotives noting that he argued that petrol had to be imported whereas coal was available in abundance, that the NER derived its revenue from coal and that if the steam locomotive was to be phased out then coal is available to generate electricity. The paper also printed a tribute from Darlington Magistrates to which the Clerk to the Court, George Watson, Raven's son-in-law responded. The *Railway Magazine* echoed much of that which was already written although it did mention that Sir Vincent was a member of the main committee of the British Engineering Standards Association. *The Times* reported the death without comment and the private obituary was a terse two-liner ending with 'No flowers by request'.

Raven's will, dated 29th May, 1931 appointed Lady Raven, Norman Raven and Leslie Pearkes (solicitor) as trustees. Probate was granted on 7th April, 1934 and shows that he left £20,036 14s. 11d. (gross), £19,453 16s. 2d. (net). The first clause was that his body should be cremated. He followed this with the following bequest,

> I bequeath to my said wife the sum of £100 for her immediate use to be paid as soon as possible after my death and I further give and bequeath to her all my jewellery, wearing apparel, wines, liquors, cigars, fuel, provisions, stores and other consumable articles absolutely.

The will then becomes bogged down in the setting up of a trust fund to provide for Lady Raven in her lifetime and with instructions that on her death all goods and chattels of which she had use 'shall form part of my residuary estate'.

Following his death, Lady Raven returned to the North East and divided her time between The Old Hall, Hurworth-on-Tees, the home of her daughter Guen and her husband and 169 George Street, London W1, the home of her son. She died in a nursing home in Devonshire Street W1 on 2nd August, 1937.

The present generation of Raven descendants. *Back row, left to right*: David Hawkins; Michael Hawkins, Raven's great-great-grandson. *Front row, left to right*: Anne Hawkins; Anne Hawkins née Watson, Raven's great-granddaughter; baby Megan, Raven's third of four great-great-great grandchildren with her aunt Denise, Raven's great-granddaughter. *Mrs Anne Hawkins*

'Q6' class No. 63395 puts up a defiant display on Seaton Bank in her final days as a BR engine.
NELPG Collection

Chapter Eleven

The Legacy

The surviving examples of Raven's locomotive design are 0-8-0 No. 2238 in the NER numbering scheme when built in December 1918 (LNER 'Q6', BR No. 63395), 0-8-0 NER No. 901 when built in 1919 (LNER 'Q7', BR No. 63460) and 'P3' class 0-6-0 NER No. 2392 when built in 1923 (LNER 'J27' BR No. 65894). It can be -and no doubt is - argued that the 0-6-0 was a Worsdell design in the same way that it can be argued that 'K1' No. 2005 is a Thompson design although Peppercorn has the credit. But the order for No. 2392 was placed in 1922 and Raven had modified the design, hence it becomes a Raven locomotive.

No. 2392 (BR 65894) was bought out of service and became the property of the newly-formed North Eastern Locomotive Preservation Group (NELPG) on 13th November, 1967 and it is to the credit of the NELPG that the purchase price was raised within a year. No. 2392 was chosen by the group for very good reasons. At £1,400 it was cheaper than an 0-8-0, it had spent most of its working life in the York area and had not been subjected to the stresses and strains experienced by its classmates working in the Durham coalfield. In addition, in March 1963 No. 2392 had been overhauled at North Road and had been given a refurbished non-superheated boiler. It worked on the last day of steam - 9th September, 1967 - following which it went to Tyne Dock depot to await collection. At the beginning of October 1967, BR 'upped the ante' to £1,800. Fortunately, the NELPG was a member of the Association of Locomotive Preservation Societies (ARPS) and through the good offices of the ARPS the original purchase price was honoured.

Many - if not all - of the Country's preservation movements have discovered that buying the locomotive, once the funds were raised, was the easy part of the project. Having parted with the money what do you do with several tons of locomotive? The former NER line from Pickering to Grosmont that was taken over in 1968 by the North Yorkshire Moors Railway Preservation Society (NYMR) was considered to be the ideal location for No. 2392 and a good working relationship was created between the two organizations. Unfortunately, at the time there were no facilities for overhaul and the only undercover storage was Grosmont tunnel. Additionally, the Tyne Dock depot was falling apart and was scheduled for demolition although some remedial work was undertaken before the engine was moved to the National Coal Board's (NCB) depot at Philadelphia near Durham where an extensive overhaul was carried out. As the NCB phased out repairs to its fleet of steam locomotives, 65894 was on the move again, this time to the BR depot at Thornaby and then in January 1971 it went to ICI Billingham whence it emerged in October 1971 dressed in NER freight livery of black lined out in red. It was steamed on 16th October, 1971 and a week later it went to Grosmont where it was handed over on loan to the North Yorkshire Moors Railway. It continued to work over the NYMR until in 1977 the NELPG was approached by the National Railway Museum with a view to 65894 - by now having reverted to its NER No. 2392 -

In preservation and restored at Grosmont on the North Yorkshire Moors Railway in October 1971 are 'Q6' class No. 3395 and 'J27' class 0-6-0 No. 2392.   *John Hunt*

A three-quarter view of 'T2' class 0-8-0 No. 2238 taken in the roundhouse at Thornaby in December 1978. The companion locomotive is 'K1' class 2-6-0 No. 2005.   *John Hunt*

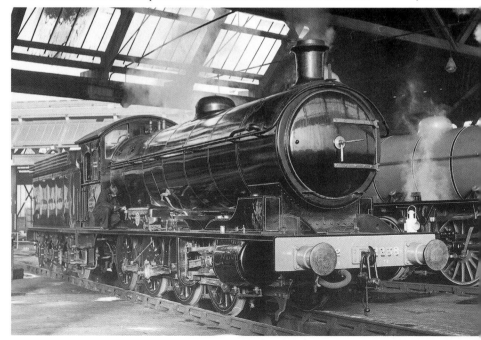

joining the National Collection on loan for a three year period. This offer was fortuitous as the boiler needed re-tubing and it was likely to be out of service for some time. The locomotive was repainted to exhibition standard and transported to York by road in October 1977.

Having successfully secured No. 65984, the NELPG turned its attention to Raven class 'T2' (no doubt about its genesis). The best of the few that remained in service was deemed to be NER No. 2238 - it was the last of the class to be overhauled at North Road in 1965. Following withdrawal, the engine was sent to Tyne Dock and arrangements were made with BR to store it until June 1968 when the purchase would be completed at an agreed price of £2,100. Once again, BR pulled the rug from under the NELPG. In a letter dated 5th December, 1967, the Group was informed, without ceremony or sensitivity, that the locomotive was no longer available as it had been sold for scrap by competitive tender. It was due to be towed to the scrap yard on the following day but fortunately the rostered crew failed to report for work - some suggestion of a heavy night - and negotiations with Hughes, Bolckow, the scrap merchants and with BR were very quickly put in hand. The purchase price had risen to £2,300 and this was raised in six months and No. 2238 (BR 63395) passed into the ownership of the NELPG on 1st April, 1968. It was moved from Tyne Dock to Hartlepool and within four months of arriving, the depot was declared unsafe - No. 2238 was on the move again this time to Thornaby roundhouse where it was joined by No. 65984.

As many enthusiasts have discovered to their cost, preservation is one thing - restoration is very different. In the case of Nos. 63395 and 65984 however those concerned with returning the locomotives to working order knew exactly what they were up against and budgeted accordingly. As a result of this enthusiastic but essentially level-headed approach coupled with hard work and dedication No. 63395 was successfully steamed at Thornaby on 18th October, 1969. The following summer, the NYMR was short of motive power and in response to a cry for help, No. 63395 was hauled in light steam from Thornaby to Grosmont on 25th June, 1970 and subsequently became the first ever ex-NER 'T2' to haul a passenger train. The locomotive worked regularly on the NYMR until 1982 when it was withdrawn for heavy repairs. Since entering the works, much time, effort and money have been expended on No. 63395. In fact the catalogue of work carried out in the past three years has all the makings of a gothic novel and underlines the point already made that there is a vast gulf between preservation and restoration. During the £100,000 overhaul of the boiler and firebox and the fitting of a new smokebox, the wheels were dropped revealing excessive wear in the motion and brakegear and in the horns and axleboxes. And so it goes on – metal stitching was required for each cylinder and for the smokebox saddle and then – there was the tender. The above skims the surface but it does emphasise just what can be done with determination and the dedication of a band of volunteers.

The third example of Raven's designs that has been preserved is NER 'T3' class 0-8-0 No. 901 (LNER 'Q7', BR 63460.) As new No. 901 went to Blaydon: in 1923 it was transferred to Hull where it stayed until 1929 when it went back to the North East where it spent the next 28 years, ending its days on the Tyne Dock - Consett iron ore trains. It was withdrawn in December 1962 but as it had been earmarked for preservation it was stored at Darlington North Road. It was

A superb view of three of the locomotives of the North Eastern Railway Preservation Group, 'T2' class 0-8-0 No. 2238, 'P3' class 0-6-0 No. 2392 and 'K1' class 2-6-0 No. 2005, passing Guisborough Junction, Middlesbrough *en route* from Thornaby to Grosmont, 22nd December, 1975. The backdrop of Middlesbrough Docks and the transporter bridge give the photograph a period feel.   *John Hunt*

repainted and in September 1963 No. 63460 worked a Stephenson Locomotive Society five day tour over the South Shields-Consett-Lanchester lines and it was out again in May 1964 when it worked a Railway Correspondence & Travel Society special from Middlesbrough to Newcastle. What happened next illustrates just how British Railways could put itself out if it so chose. In stark contrast to its cavalier attitude towards the NELPG and the purchase of No. 63395, during the 13 years that followed the RCTS special, No. 63460 was re-located four times - Darlington, Stratford East, Hellifield and Brighton. Whilst at Brighton the locomotive was examined and was found to be sound and intact. (So was every locomotive that came out of Barry - at least that is what the reports implied!)

In 1978 No. 63460 was moved again, this time to York. The NRM and the NELPG came to an agreement over the locomotive's future and in April 1978 it went to the NYMR on a 10 year loan, with the NELPG being responsible for its restoration.*

Coach Preservation

The North Eastern Railway Coach Group (NERCG) was founded in 1971 and has, over the intervening years, acquired three former NER coaches - autocar No. 3453, a 52ft-long clerestory coach built in 1905; No. 945, a 52 ft open third corridor built in 1924 and the third vehicle, not strictly owned by the NERCG; is owned by members within the parent group and is a six-wheeled 32 ft-long luggage composite built in 1880.

---

* From information kindly supplied by John Hunt, Chairman, NELPG.

Chapter Twelve

Raven Miscellany

Raven Fog Signalling Apparatus

This was a system of automatic train control and was especially beneficial in foggy weather. The apparatus, developed by Raven and Charlie Baister, was introduced in 1894.

> It consisted of a rising arm in the four foot connected by a rod or wire with the home or distant signals so that when the signal is at danger, this arm, being erect is struck by a shoe on the engine causing a whistle to sound in the cab also slightly applying the Westinghouse brake until released by the driver.

This is the official description of the equipment taken from a letter dated 21st October, 1920 and addressed to the Ministry of Transport. The Ministry had expressed interest and enquired into the reliability of the system. Raven and Baister patented it in 1896 and the company was so pleased with it that it was eventually fitted, with modifications, to 1,488 locomotives irrespective of the type of brake.

Doubts were expressed about the efficiency of the equipment, particularly with respect to the vulnerability of the rising arm - it was thought that it might be snapped off. This did not happen because Raven specified lightweight, flexible arms and failures were rare.

The letter referred to above enquired in depth into the use of the apparatus with a view to its being adopted countrywide. It seems, however, that the Ministry had problems with the vocabulary. The company replied in detail supplying reports from every grade of employee involved with the apparatus and supplied details of failures for the years 1917, 1918 and 1919. These were as follows - 1917 - 18 failures; 1918 seven failures (all broken arms); 1919 - 10 failures. The reply, whilst acknowledging the information, asked for explanations of the meanings of 'total track mileage' and 'number of locomotives'. There had been a feasibility study in November 1919 under Col Pringle but a letter dated 19th August, 1921 and addressed to all railway companies advised them not to proceed with installing the equipment, despite the fact that it had worked satisfactorily for the North Eastern for several years and that it eventually covered the main line from Shaftholme Junction to Berwick.

In addition to the above, Raven developed an electrical version of the apparatus. This consisted of ramps between and outside the rails coming into contact with a wire brush and a rotary switch on the locomotive. It was installed in 1907 and 20 locomotives were fitted at a cost of £340 each. It was updated in 1911 and gave indications of the position of home and distant signals at junctions and on the main line. This version did not last as long as did the mechanical version and was abandoned after some 10 years.

Raven and the North British Railway

In 1907 Raven was seconded to the North British Railway as the company was having problems with its Atlantics. The background to Raven's involvement is a sorry tale of Chief Officer in-fighting, personality clashes and a General Manager, William Fulton Jackson, who was an out and out bully. In 1903 W.P. Reid was, much to his surprise, appointed locomotive superintendent and set to work on designs for a big engine that would eliminate the necessity for double-heading over the tortuous routes with which the NBR was blessed. He was aware that Ivatt (GNR), Robinson (GCR), Worsdell (NER) and Marsh (LBSCR) were busy developing the Atlantic type and he had no desire to be left behind. The result of his labours was No. 868, named *Aberdonian*, which had its inaugural run on 1st July, 1906 and was the prototype of a further 14. The Civil Engineer, James Bell, was not enamoured of the new class. He maintained that the locomotives were top heavy and that they damaged the track and any class of steam locomotive thus accused was as much of a Pariah as a fast bowler accused of throwing and the Reid Atlantics were withdrawn. This threw the Board into disarray to the extent that it seriously considered disposing of the Atlantics - the most expensive locomotives to run on the system - less than a year after they were introduced. But were not the Atlantics the company's prestige locomotives and had not their withdrawal played havoc with both freight and passenger services? At this point Jackson, the General Manager, involved himself. Typically and without a by your leave, he contacted Oliver Bury, General Manager of the Great Northern, enquiring whether or not H.A. Ivatt could be spared in an attempt to solve the problems that were being encountered. At the time, Ivatt was regarded - certainly by Jackson - as the guru of British Atlantics. Bury was prepared to help a fellow GM and in due course Ivatt was released by the GNR. Again, typical of Jackson's attitude, 10 days elapsed before he informed Reid that Ivatt was involved. Modifications in addition to those already made by Reid were suggested by Ivatt but the Board in its wisdom rejected Ivatt's main recommendation - that the Atlantics should be restricted to 55 mph 'with the consequent adverse effect on the operating department' - on the strength of an analysis produced by Dr James Inglis, who was not only the Director responsible for locomotive matters but was also on the Board of his family firm of shipbuilders. There is no record of how Ivatt felt about what could be considered as a snub but he was paid 100 guineas for his trouble.

Jackson next contacted A. Kaye Butterworth of the NER in May 1907 and in the meantime, the in-fighting continued. James Bell, the Civil Engineer who lived for his job and was paranoid about what he referred to as 'his track' committed a cardinal sin by writing direct to Reid with a list of complaints and not via Jackson. Surprisingly, however, Jackson forgave Bell and turned on Reid whom he always treated with thinly veiled contempt. It was averred that as built, the Atlantics were 'rogue engines, disconcerting to drivers, terror to civil engineers' Jackson wrote to Reid and implied that unless the troubles on the line were cleared up then Reid might be looking for another job. He also wrote to Reid demanding - not requesting - that Reid be present at meetings that he,

Jackson, decreed to be important and excuses would not be tolerated. The outcome was that Raven was brought in as temporary consulting engineer and at the end of May he met Reid and Bell in Edinburgh having first familiarized himself with the information that they had supplied. Raven was satisfied that the NBR Atlantics were more than equal to the job for which they were designed and he recommended modifications to the valves. Reid was authorized to send one of his fitters to Gateshead to obtain details of Raven's proposals and it was agreed that he - Raven -would return to Edinburgh for three days in June. Whilst there, it was arranged that he would travel on the footplate the 98 miles from Carlisle to Edinburgh, be on the footplates of other members of the class and supervise a run from Edinburgh to Newcastle and return using the NER dynamometer car. The culmination of this frenetic activity was the presentation of his findings and his recommendations to the NBR Directors.

Raven arrived at Carlisle on the afternoon of Monday, 10th June to discover that the modifications that he had recommended had not been completed and thus, the locomotive selected, *Waverley*, was not available. History records that Bell was not best pleased but, unfortunately, Raven does not refer to the incident in his diary. He travelled the route the following day and realised the difficulties that the 98 miles posed to NBR locomotives. It is a heavily-graded route with climbs of 1 in 80 and 1 in 70 at Whitrope and Fallahill and the sharp climb from Edinburgh to Portobello On the Wednesday the dynamometer car was attached to the 10.10 am from Edinburgh to Newcastle with the return working at 3.36 pm with No. 879 *Abbotsford* in charge in each direction.

Raven submitted a report dated 18th June, 1907 to the Chairman and Directors of the NBR. The report is, uncharacteristically, sycophantic. He lists the seven locomotives on which he rode noting that *Abbotsford* was the best and that *Liddlesdale* the worst in coping with what he describes as the 'curvey' nature of the Waverley route. He found no evidence of irregular tyre wear - had this been the case it would have revealed damage to the track. He comments on the performance of *Abbotsford* on the Edinburgh-Newcastle and expressed himself perfectly satisfied with the performance of the locomotive at speeds of up to 80 mph. He further comments that the NER pilot driver who was on the footplate from Berwick to Newcastle and return was similarly satisfied.

He noted that the big ends were inclined to run hot and that he considered the coal consumption - eight tons used on the Newcastle-Edinburgh round trip - to be excessive. His remedy for the former was a better quality of oil than that that was in use and for the latter, adjustments to the piston valves.

He ends the report by gilding the lily. He states that the seven locomotives did very good work and were equal to any similar locomotives anywhere in the country and that included the NER.

The print-outs of the runs no longer exist and it is not possible to come to any conclusions. Raven was again in Carlisle for the 3.50 pm Edinburgh on 10th July following which he proposed changes to the piston rings. These modifications were carried out and he repeated the Carlisle - Edinburgh run on 2nd August, 1907. In September Reid reported to the NBR Board on the success of the trials and he was authorised to modify the entire stud of Atlantics. Additionally,

Worsdell/Smith '4CC' class compound 4-4-2 No. 731 on 22nd August, 1931. Introduced in 1908 it was withdrawn in 1933.

John Clewley Collection

Raven was of the opinion that the Aberdeen block trains should be re-timed and thus slowed - this too was accepted by the Board and Raven, his reputation enhanced was 200 guineas better off. Not everyone was happy, however and William Fulton Jackson sought help from the Midland Railway and borrowed a Deeley compound for trials on the Waverley route. In May 1908 he wrote to Butterworth asking the NER Board to approve the loan of an NER compound. As a result of the request, No. 730 worked the 10.30 am Edinburgh-Carlisle on 2nd June, 1908 with inspector McLellan on the footplate. Unfortunately No. 730 stalled on the approach to the climb to Whitrope and in trying to get the train on the move she slipped violently and had to be taken off. No. 730 was replaced in August 1908 and on the 11th August No. 731 was on the same working - the 10.30 am Edinburgh-Carlisle returning with the 3.55 pm. McLellan ensured that there was no repetition of No. 730's antics although on the 14th, No. 731 blew a gland on the right-hand high pressure cylinder and this signalled the end of the affair. No. 731 was returned to its rightful owners and the NBR abandoned thoughts of compound propulsion and stuck to building Atlantics one of which - *Highland Chief* (LNER No. 9902) - took part in the 1925 Stockton & Darlington Railway Centenary celebrations. The last Atlantic built by and for any British railway was turned out of Cowlairs works in 1921.

'T3' Locomotives at Work

As it is almost 40 years since any of Raven's locomotives were in revenue earning service and as it has not been possible to locate former drivers and firemen who worked on them reliance has to be placed on contemporary amateur accounts. O.S. Nock records in graphic detail a footplate trip on a 'T3',

It is here that the fearful climb up to Consett begins in grim earnest. Another 'T3' buffered up in rear and after an exchange of whistle signals we were away. Then, for 35 minutes I saw a big engine worked as near to absolutely all-out as one was likely to see anywhere. The regulator was full open and the reverser only one notch from full gear.

The roar of the exhaust was music in the ears of a locomotive man and looking back on the curves I could see from the way the exhaust from the banking engine was shooting skywards from her chimney that she too was being well and truly thrashed. But this is the kind of work for which these engines were designed.

. . . and just beyond Beamish there is a pronounced easing of the gradient for about half a mile. There was no easing of the locomotives. Both of them were allowed to charge away to nearly 30 mph. The roar of the three cylinder exhaust was indescribable. And it was just at that moment when the rate of steaming had been more than doubled that the safety valves blew off. Still the gauge showed a full glass of water and it seemed as though this amazing engine could have sustained this effort indefinitely.

Middlesbrough Dock

The River Tees marks the boundary between the counties of Cleveland and South Durham and has had various changes of fortune down the centuries - if a river can be said to have fortunes. In medieval times there was a trade in lead that was mined in the Pennines and brought by road to the river at Worsall and exported. Yarm, with its impressive High Street (and now with an equally impressive NER viaduct) was an important port for trade with Europe, that is, until someone decided to build a bridge across the river at Stockton in 1771 and this had the effect of a decline in trade at Yarm and, of course, an increase in trade at Stockton. In 1808 the Tees Navigation Company was formed and in 1810 shortened the distance from Stockton to the sea by over two miles with the construction of the Mandale Cut.

The Stockton & Darlington Railway Company's plans to convey coal from the South Durham Coalfield received Royal Assent and the line from Witton Park to Stockton was opened on 27th September, 1825. All was not well with traders using the Tees as it could, on occasions, take ships several days to reach Stockton from the sea. In response to the disquiet, the S&DR decided to construct an extension about four miles in length from Stockton to a point about seven miles from the sea. The end of the line was named Port Darlington, a name that did not meet with the approval of the Stockton traders and did not survive as a name. In 1829, Thomas Richardson purchased 520 acres of land on the south side of the river for £30,000. He was joined by Joseph Pease, his brother Edward and with other relatives they formed a company to develop the site - it was known variously as Pease & Partners or the Owners of the Middlesbrough Estate (OME) - and from the purchase grew Middlesbrough and Middlesbrough Dock. According to the *Durham Chronicle*, 1st January, 1831, a new town was planned to be 'a place of great trade and opulence'.

By 1838 trade was being inhibited by variations in the depth of the water at the coal staithes and the S&DR was anxious to construct an enclosed dock but was prevented from so doing by the conditions of its Act of Parliament. The OME stepped in and offered to finance the project on the condition that the S&DR would ship all the OME's coal traffic - this was not a problem to the S&DR. So much for the background.

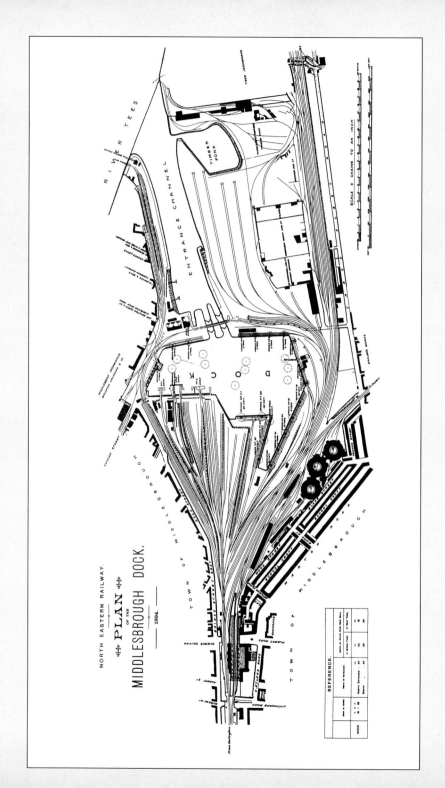

NORTH EASTERN RAILWAY.

PLAN
OF THE
MIDDLESBROUGH DOCK.
1894

SCALE 3 CHAINS TO AN INCH

The original dock was laid out by William Cubitt in 1839 and it was opened in May 1842. In 1849 the S&DR obtained an Act of Parliament that effectively transferred the ownership from the OME to the S&DR and then in 1863 the S&DR was absorbed into the NER. Edward Fletcher was quite happy with the status quo and although the NER now owned the dock it operated separately and was managed by the 'Darlington Committee'. It was under this committee that the first extension was laid out to the designs of T.E. Harrison, Chief Engineer of the NER. The construction was completed in 1874 and had the effect of increasing the acreage in the dock from nine to 12. Minute 6882 dated 20th November, 1874 awarded £500 to W.J. Cudworth - Harrison's assistant - 'as a bonus for work undertaken at Middlesbrough Dock'. Unfortunately. the minutes do not reveal what Cudworth had done to deserve his bonus. Four years later, Harrison was back at his drawing board and was at work on a second extension that took eight years to complete and increased the area to 15 acres at a cost of £200,000. Minute 8993 dated 11th January, 1884 reveals that the Tees Conservancy Commissioners - who succeeded the Tees Navigation Company in 1852 - wrote to the NER requesting that the proposed enlargement should be delayed. The company replied to the effect that contract stage had not been reached. Obviously it was reached and the work proceeded. T.E. Harrison died in office in 1888 following which three engineering divisions were formed - North, Central and Southern. W.J. Cudworth was appointed engineer for the Southern Division in 1899, a post that he held for 10 years.

In 1897 powers to enlarge the dock were granted and the work was carried out between 1897 and 1902. This was the final enlargement and the dock retained its size - 25 acres - and shape to the end of its working life and coincided with a paper that Raven produced on the advantages of electrically-operated cranes over cranes that were operated hydraulically. The paper, 40 pages long of which 12 are tables, was included in the proceedings of the Institute of Mechanical Engineers in 1904. It is a typical Raven presentation reflecting his incisive thinking, attention to detail and the contents are closely argued in favour of electricity.

The opening paragraph sets the scene:

Now that the question of electric appliances for dock purposes is so generally considered, the author thinks that it may be of interest to record and place before the members of the Institute the particulars of the installation and the tests that have been made at Middlesbrough Dock on the North Eastern Railway, comparing hydraulic with electric. These are working side by side and are all thoroughly up to date, giving an excellent opportunity for judging the value of one against the other so far as economy of working is concerned.

Occasionally Raven's objectivity slips, 'Cables -The distribution of current is effected by a network of feeders and distribution cables laid below ground'. He then goes on to describe in detail water tight junction boxes and various types of equipment, ending this particular section: 'The cost of cables complete is only about 50% of the cost of hydraulic mains for the same power'.

Warming to his theme he continues, 'The Traffic Department finds the electric cranes to be a great advantage. There is little time required for oiling as the crane has ring lubricators to all main bearings and the wheels run in oil baths which only require attention once a month'.

Raven then turns his attention to savings to be made by economising in man-power, a subject dear to his heart throughout his career.

When it has been necessary to move the hydraulic cranes to suit the working into the various ships' holds, six men have had to be called one hour earlier in the morning to set the four cranes that are required for each vessel. With the electric cranes the men do not have to be called earlier as two men in summer and four in winter can connect and disconnect four cranes in fifteen minutes. In winter on frosty nights four men have been employed six hours each for the purpose of keeping fires to prevent water in the cylinders of the hydraulic cranes from freezing.

He emphasized that the electric cranes were ready for work at a moment's notice whereas the driver of a steam-operated crane had to book on duty an hour early in order to raise steam. (He used this argument some 20 years later in his steam vs electric traction report.)

But Raven did not have things all his own way. Edward B. Ellington, the Vice-President of the Institute challenged some of Raven's findings and conclusions. He pointed out that the hydraulic cranes were some 15 years old and, 'In no sense could these be taken to be comparable with the very perfect electric cranes recently erected'.

Mr John Barr took Raven to task over his statement that it took six men to move the hydraulic cranes into position ready for work. 'Why', asked Mr Barr, 'furnish the electric cranes with power motors for travelling purposes at lavish cost and deny the same privilege to hydraulic?'

He continued, 'The author of the paper having made the study of electric power as applied to dock appliances his own, he might be forgiven for being perhaps a little prejudiced in favour of electric power. This preference appeared in various parts of the paper'.

Raven's summary is interesting and is reproduced here. He was sorry that he should have conveyed to Mr Barr's mind that he was prejudiced in favour of electric power. He had had a great number of years' experience on the North Eastern Railway with all kinds of hydraulic dock machinery and considered that they had at Middlesbrough an exceptional opportunity of comparing electrical with hydraulic machinery for dock work. He therefore instituted a number of tests as near as possible under similar conditions which had been placed before the Institute and he had judged only upon these trials, which he hoped might be found of value. It was in between the second and third extensions that Raven was promoted and this brought with it responsibility for the dock machinery. On becoming CME he worked closely with two docks engineers - T.M. Newell who held the post from 1899 to 1913 and who was succeeded by Charles Watson.

It would seem, then, that with the experience gained with the Tyneside electrification scheme, with his visit to the USA and his detailed comparison of electric, hydraulic and steam cranes, all roads led to Shildon and Raven was a very willing traveller.

Epilogue

Sir Vincent Raven - A Profile

In the course of a letter written to Dr Geoffrey Hughes in July 1982 the late Willie Yeadon regretted that he was unable to put Dr Hughes in touch with anyone who knew Raven 'in any capacity'. Twenty years later and despite much time and effort being expended on research, the situation has not changed. This being so, industrial psychologist Steven Poppleton has produced the following profile of Sir Vincent:

Two questions come to mind - what was the effect of Raven's religious upbringing and why did he opt for the NER whilst his brother went to Cambridge? As there is no evidence that he was a churchgoer, it is safe to assume that his background made him anti-church. His reason for joining the NER could have been financial - were there insufficient funds to support two undergraduates - the income from the church was £552 pa - and, as was common at the time, the elder of the two took precedence?

His stable marriage and his stable career point to a strong sense of duty, loyalty and conscientiousness. He was careful, liked to do things properly and he had clear ideas of right and wrong, not only for himself but also for others - (here is a possible link to his religious upbringing) and early promotion suggests that he was a stickler for detail.

The above traits could lead to difficulty in dealing with people and his management style was likely to have been abrasive and he was probably lacking in emotional sensitivity and sensitivity to others. Engineers are often 'tough minded', realistic, no nonsense managers - masculine in style and expecting others to be equally tough - not good when others need emotional support and the various disputes in which he was involved show that he was intolerant of what he considered to be unacceptable behaviour.

His attitude towards electrification suggests persistence, determination and perhaps an obsessional rigidity of thought although there was something of the visionary about him - receptive to new ideas and a commitment to what he believed to be right.

Raven had a strong sense of duty as evidenced by serving as a councillor and college governor. Membership of a Masonic Lodge and being a JP suggests that he respected established traditions in society and had clear, traditional ideas of right and wrong. In addition, his membership of various learned societies culminating in the Presidency of the Institute of Mechanical Engineers suggest that he had the respect of his peers.

Summary

Raven's diary entries and management style reveal a cold rational person who was highly intelligent, had difficulty in relating to people and in all probability preferred things to people. On the other hand, his stable family life suggests a well adjusted individual who coped well with life's trials.

Appendix

Vincent Raven's Locomotives

Class	Type	First Batch	Subsequent Batches	No. Built	LNER Class
Steam Locomotives					
T2	0-8-0	1913	1917-1921	120	Q6
T3	0-8-0	1919	1924	15	Q7
Z/Z1	4-4-2	1911	1914-1918	50	C7
D	4-4-4T *	1913/4	1920-2	45	H1
S2	4-6-0	1911/2	1912/3	20	B15
S3	4-6-0	1919/20	1920-1924	70	B16
Y	4-6-2T	1910/1		20	A7
4.6.2	4-6-2	1922	1924	5	A2
		No. of steam locomotives		345	
Electric Locomotives					
Shildon-Erimus 1,100 hp	Bo-Bo	1914	1919	10	EB1 †
No. 13	2-Co-2	1922		1	
		No. of electric locomotives		11	
		Grand total		356	

Notes

* Between 1931 and 1936 all members of the class were rebuilt as 4-6-2Ts and reclassified by the LNER as 'A8'.

† Not classified until 4th October, 1945. One member of the class, No. 11, was converted for use as a banking engine on the Manchester-Sheffield-Wath line in 1942, but in fact was sent to work on the ex-Great Eastern suburban electrification scheme. In 1949 No. 11 retained the class designation 'EB1', while its sister engines were reclassified as 'EF1'.

Bibliography

Allen, C.J., *British Pacific Locomotives*, Ian Allan, 1962.

Allen, C.J., *North Eastern Railway*, Ian Allan, 1964.

Brown, F.A.S., *Nigel Gresley: Locomotive Engineer*, Ian Allan, 1961.

Hennessey, R.A.S., *The Electric Railway That Never Was, York-Newcastle 1919*, Oriel Press, 1970.

Hoole, Ken, *Electric Locomotives of the North Eastern Railway*, Oakwood Press, 1988.

Hoole, Ken, *An Illustrated History of NER Locomotives*, Oxford Publishing Co., 1988.

Hughes, Dr Geoffrey, *LNER*, Ian Allan, 1986.

Hughes, Dr Geoffrey, *Sir Nigel Gresley: the Engineer and his Family*, Oakwood Press, 2001.

Jackson, David, *J.G. Robinson, A Lifetime's Work*, Oakwood Press, 1996.

Nock, O.S., *Locomotives of the North Eastern Railway*, Ian Allan, 1954.

Nock, O.S., *From the Footplate, Reminiscences of the Last Days of Steam*, Granada, 1984

Proud, John H., *The History of the Middlesbrough Dock*: 1842-2000, published privately 2000.

Thomas, John, *The North British Railway*, David & Charles, 1969.

Townend, P.N., *East Coast Pacifics at Work*, Ian Allan, 1982.

Tuplin, W.A., *North Eastern Steam*, George Allen & Unwin, 1970.

Proceedings of the Institute of Electrical Engineers pp.787-827; June 1904.

Various issues of *The North Eastern Express*, the journal of the North Eastern Railway Association.

Various volumes of *Locomotives of the LNER*, RCTS.

Peppercorn 'A1' Pacific No. 60126 *Sir Vincent Raven*.   *Clive Field Archive*

Index